P O W E R P A C K

Training manual

Teaching foundations and practical applications
for working with children

First published in 2000 by
KEVIN MAYHEW LTD
Buxhall
Stowmarket
Suffolk IP14 3BW

© 2000 Powerpack

0 1 2 3 4 5 6 7 8 9

ISBN 1 84003 637 0
Catalogue No 1500387

Cover design by Jonathan Stroulger
Illustrations by Sally-Anne Norman
Edited and typeset by Elisabeth Bates
Printed in Great Britain

Contents

Introduction

This manual is particularly for those working with 5-11 year olds, although many of the principles also apply to 3-5s. It is a comprehensive but not exhaustive guide to children's ministry – there is obviously always more to learn and God is also constantly doing new things!

Many years of experience in all kinds of children's ministry situations have formed the basis for this manual which began its life as notes used on Powerpack training courses. It is divided into two sections. The first consists of a number of foundational subjects, while the second contains information, practical helps and ideas on a whole range of different aspects of children's ministry.

The manual can be used as a reference book by an individual or as the basis for training and discussion for groups of children's workers. At the end of many of the sections there are exercises with the purpose of encouraging the application of the teaching into particular church situations.

Many revivals have started by God pouring his Spirit out on children and young people. We, too, are living in exciting times, where there are signs of revival in different places throughout the world. If this manual enables people to minister more effectively to children, thereby creating an environment in which God can move powerfully and freely, then it will have achieved its purpose.

Acknowledgements

The publishers wish to express their gratitude to the following copyright owners who have granted permission to include their copyright material in this book.

Jackie Cray and CPAS, Athena Drive, Tachbrook Park, Warwick, CV34 6NG, for the extracts from *Seen and Heard* by Jackie Cray.

Destiny Image Publishers, 167 Walnut Bottom Road, Shippensburg, PA 17257, USA, for the extracts from *Soldiers with Little Feet* by Dian Layton.

Evangelical Press, Grange Close, Faverdale North Industrial Estate, Darlington, DL3 0PH, for the extract from *Revival!* by Brian Edwards.

Good News Ministries, 220 Sleepy Creek Road, Macon, Georgia 31210, USA, for the extract from *Children Aflame* by David Walters (Phone: 912 757 8071, E-mail: goodnews@hom.net, Website: www.goodnews.netministries.org).

Group Publishing Inc., Dept. BK, PO Box 481, Loveland, CO 80539, USA, for the extract from *The Discipline Guide for Children's Ministry* by Jody Capehart and Gordon and Becki West, © 1997.

Monarch Publications, Broadway House, Crowborough, East Sussex, TN6 1HQ, for the extracts from *And For Your Children* by Chris and John Leach.

Scripture Union, 207-209 Queensway, Bletchley, Milton Keynes, Bucks, MK2 2EB for extracts from *Dear God, Can You Wink?* By Gillian Raymond, and *Storytelling: A Practical Guide* by Lance Pierson. Used by permission.

Section 1
Foundations

Children – VIPs

If the Kingdom of God is to come in power, we must start with the children and teach them from the very cradle. Martin Luther

TODAY NOT TOMORROW

Children are an important part of the church TODAY – the potential leaders of TOMORROW! Most church congregations contain a good percentage of children and yet in many cases the children's work is still the 'Cinderella' of church life. Could this be because the church does not fully appreciate the spiritual potential and contribution of children for NOW?

In his book, *Kids in Combat* (Good News Ministries), David Walters shares a vision he received in which a large army of adults were seen standing in ranks, prepared for battle. Behind them were a scattered group of children and teenagers looking uninvolved and disinterested. He concludes that this is the state of many of our churches. The Lord was then seen to come and part the ranks of adult soldiers, drawing the children forward into the ranks with the adults.

God wants to use children today! He wants them to be discipled, trained and released in ministry, rather than just 'looked after', entertained or taught at a superficial level.

Tragically, in normal church life we have a low spiritual expectation for our children. We do not expect much from them because we do not expect much from ourselves . . . One generation creates the environment that either stifles or invigorates the spiritual growth of the next. (*Revival!* by Brian Edwards, Evangelical Press)

The time has come for us to redress this situation, to allow God to give us his vision and raise our expectations. Then we will be able to create an environment where children can reach their full spiritual potential – strong in God, confident and effective in ministry.

WHAT DOES THE BIBLE SAY?

1. *Children by nature are sinful* (Genesis 8:21; Psalm 51:5; 58:3; Proverbs 29:15).

2. *Children are to be greatly valued* (Psalm 127:3-4; Matthew 18:1-6, 10-11; 19:13-15; Luke 18:15-16).

3. *Children need to be taught* (Exodus 10:1-2; Deuteronomy 4:9; 6:6-7; 32:46; Psalm 78:4-6; Proverbs 22:6; Ephesians 6:4).

   In Judges 2:7 we read that 'The people served the Lord throughout the lifetime of Joshua and of the elders who outlived him and who had seen all the great things the Lord had done for Israel.'

   But in verse 10 of the same chapter there is a very sad state of affairs reported: 'After that whole generation had been gathered to their fathers, another generation grew up, who knew neither the Lord nor what he had done for Israel.'

   This was the result of children not being taught about the Lord and sadly it is also an accurate description of the situation in our day and age.

4. *Children need to be disciplined* (Proverbs 13:24; 19:18; 22:15; 23:13).

5. *Children need to be included* (Deuteronomy 29:10-13; 31:12-13; Nehemiah 8:2; Ezra 10:1; Jonah 4:11; Acts 2:38-39).

6. God wants to use children, e.g. Samuel (1 Samuel 3:1ff); Daniel (in Daniel, chapter 1, Daniel was probably only 14 years old!); Naaman's servant girl; Josiah, the boy with the five loaves and two fishes.

IT'S ALL BEEN SAID BEFORE!

Charles H. Spurgeon said,

Your Sunday schools are admirable; but what is their purpose if you do not teach the Gospel in them? You get children together and keep them quiet for an hour-and-a-half and then send them home; but what is the good of it? It may bring some quiet to their fathers and mothers, and that is, perhaps, why they send them to the school; but all the real good lies in what is taught the children. The most fundamental should be prominent; and what is this but the Cross.

Be not content to sow principles in their minds which may possibly develop in after years, but be working for immediate conversion. Expect fruit in your children while they are children.

Francis Xavier (sixteenth-century Spanish Jesuit missionary) said,

Give me a child until he is seven, and you can do what you like with him afterwards.

Lenin said,

Give me four years to teach the children, and the seed I have sown will never be uprooted.

CHILDREN, PARENTS AND THE CHURCH

The responsibility for the bringing up of children belongs to the parents. The church is, or should be just a back-up. The ideal is a partnership between parents and the church with children's leaders being the link in this. Supporting parents and making recommendations should all be part of the job of children's leaders.

Communication with parents is vital. It is important that they know what is happening in the children's ministry and that they reinforce it at home and vice versa. With 8760 hours in a year and maybe only a maximum of 50 hours in church there is a limit to what can be done with children if their parents are not involved in the process. (Obviously in the case of children from non-Christian homes, leaders need to be *in loco*

parentis to them and do all that they can to provide the spiritual input that the children need.

A newsletter produced by the children's leaders for the parents at fairly regular intervals (once a term maybe) is a good way of communicating information to parents. Also the appropriateness of current TV programmes, books, toys, etc., could be highlighted as well as positive recommendations from parents.

Organising a Children's Ministry open evening can also provide the opportunity for parents and children's leaders to meet to talk about the spiritual progress and needs of the children.

Link up a child with a Christian adult, who will commit themselves to pray for that child. The child's photograph could be given to this person to act as a reminder. Encourage the child and its parents to pass on prayer requests. As well as meaning that all the children in the church are covered in prayer it can also help build relationships between children and adults. This also serves to give adults who are not involved in the children's ministry a focus on children. (Of course there is also the option that the children could commit themselves to pray for 'their adult'.)

Exercise 1
Do a study on what the Bible says about children.

Exercise 2
Think about how the children's ministry in your church could be given more prominence.

Vision and values

VISION

Agreeing on a common vision for the children's work in any church is essential. Where are we going? What do we want to achieve with the children? Without this, it may not be long before there is confusion about goals, disillusionment and a general sense of apathy. The vision needs to be worked out in agreement with the church leaders. This will mean looking at the overall vision of the church and reflecting something of that in the children's work. A vision statement needs to be produced and 'owned' by the whole church. In that way the congregation will be more 'on board' with all that happens in the children's work. Parents in particular need to know what the vision for the children's ministry in the church is and have the opportunity to discuss any points with which they are not happy.

What do children need?

An understanding of what children need will help determine the vision. Then a strategy needs to be decided upon, which will enable the vision to be worked out in practice.

Children need to:

1. Know the Scriptures.

2. Encounter God in salvation.

3. Experience God through his Holy Spirit.

4. Know his ways.

5. Be encouraged to apply what they learn to their everyday lives.

6. Be taught how and given opportunities to worship and pray.

7. Develop their own ministries within the Body of Christ.

8. Be taught how to discern right from wrong, good from evil in today's society, e.g. in the media.

9. Feel secure, loved and valued.

10. Discover that meeting with God is easy, exciting and enjoyable.

11. Build good relationships with one another as well as with their leaders.

12. Be encouraged to look 'outwards' in mission and evangelism.

VALUES

Values affect what we think and, consequently, what we do. Our values are an intrinsic part of us, although we seldom think about them in a conscious fashion. They determine the ideas, principles, and concepts a person or group can accept, assimilate, remember, and transmit. They can be fallible and must be constantly revised and reviewed in the light of Scripture.
(John Wimber)

God has called us to do our very best in our work for him and because of this there are a number of things that are foundational and vital to the way in which we conduct any meetings with children. Below are the set of values that we have adopted in the ministry that I lead. They could form the basis for any work amongst children but each individual church group needs to agree their own values, i.e. which ones are non-negotiable and which are not.

1. Conducive environment

a. The room should be clean, have suitable flooring, lighting, be at the right temperature, etc.

b. Equipment should be safe and of good quality.

c. A first aid kit should be readily accessible.

d. There should be plenty of colour, e.g. banners, children's artwork.

e. There should be an atmosphere of love and acceptance, faith and expectancy.

2. Good organisation and preparation

a. Be ready in plenty of time.

b. Think and plan ahead for potential problem areas, e.g. the beginning and ending of sessions, quizzes, games, etc.

c. Rules need to be agreed upon and consistently adhered to by both leaders and children.

d. Everything must be fair. For instance, if the

children are divided into teams they should be as equal as possible.

e. Adequate prayer cover is vital.

3. Fast moving programme

a. There should be just one main theme to communicate, with the different ingredients of the programme reinforcing it.

b. Concentration span awareness. Children can concentrate at an optimum level for one minute per year of their age.

c. There needs to be a balance of activity, standing/sitting, listening/doing, serious/fun. The more variety the better.

d. The different ingredients of the programme need to flow together, with no gaps. It is best if one person holds it all together.

4. Fun

a. Use humour wherever possible, e.g. in puppet and drama sketches.

b. Play games, and include craft projects, etc, which do not have any spiritual content, but are just fun!

5. Team

a. All team members should be called by God.

b. There needs to be one shared vision.

c. Good, open, regular communication is vital.

d. Team members should honour others above themselves.

e. There needs to be one overall leader.

6. Teaching

a. All teaching needs to biblically based.

b. Visual aids need to be used.

c. Variety in teaching methods is vital.

7. Praise, worship and prayer

a. These should be seen as vehicles to bring children into contact with God.

b. They should have an adventurous feel about them.

c. There should be as much variety as possible.

d. Leaders should be good models!

8. Challenge, response and ministry

a. There should be frequent challenge given as regards salvation, being filled with the Spirit, lifestyle, etc.

b. Whenever possible there should be a time for response and ministry.

9. Equipping and discipling

a. Every opportunity should be used to make disciples – children that are strong in God and are prepared to really follow him.

b. There needs to be an emphasis on both equipping for ministry and for life.

c There needs to be a relaxed and accepting atmosphere. Children need to know that they can make a mistake as regards using the gifts of the Spirit, for example, and not be judged for it. Instead they need to be encouraged to try again until they get it right.

d. Children's gifts and ministries need to be identified and encouraged.

10. Pastoral care

a. Opportunity needs to be given for children to share their problems and to receive counselling and prayer.

b. Children need to be in small groups so that a leader can adequately care for them.

Inclusive not exclusive

In Mark 10, verses 13ff, we read,

People were bringing little children to Jesus to have him touch them, but the disciples rebuked them. When Jesus saw this, he was indignant. He said to them, 'Let the little children come to me, and do not hinder them, for the kingdom of God belongs to such as these. . . .' And he took the children in his arms, put his hands on them and blessed them.

Jesus was at this point nearing the end of his earthly ministry – time was precious but still he took the time to bless this group of children. The disciples on the other hand, despite Jesus' earlier teaching in Mark 9, verses 36ff, were wanting to keep the children from Jesus.

Jesus' attitude was inclusive, the disciples' exclusive. The same is true in many of our churches today. We say that children should be included in the life of the church, but often the things we actually do or don't do have an exclusive effect.

In Old Testament times too, children were very much part of the religious life of the Jewish people. They were involved in times of national repentance (Ezra 10:1), of national rejoicing (Nehemiah 12:43), at times when the law was read publicly (Deuteronomy 31:12), etc.

Children need to know that they are accepted as important members of the church. They need to see and experience this rather than just hear it. Jackie Cray writes in her book, *Seen and Heard*, that children

have a right to belong. The kingdom of God belongs to them and they are to be cherished, protected and nurtured in God's family in his world. They are of unique significance and are therefore to be welcomed . . . They are to be attended to, not by extra-curricular activities, but by the whole church family . . . Our children

belong in a web of relationships which includes young and old, single and married. These relationships will be shaped by the experience of the cross of Christ. They will be founded on costly commitment and servanthood.

Our churches need to become much more 'child-friendly', creating an environment of inclusion, a sense of 'we are in this together'. This is not just about what we do in our church services and activities but about attitudes, about vision, about behaviour, etc. We need to work hard at making church a place where children want to go, a place where they can feel secure enough to let God impact their lives.

There are three main ways in which we can exclude children:

1. By what we expect of them

Too often our spiritual expectations for children are very low and as a result we do not include them in the heart of the spiritual life of the church. For example, do we expect them to hear from God? Do we expect them to intercede? Do we expect them to worship in 'spirit and in truth'? If we do, then opportunity needs to be given for these things to happen. They have all the spiritual potential of adults and need to be given the same opportunity to minister.

2. By how we behave towards them

a. Ignoring them.
Imagine a situation in which a mother arrives at the door of the church with her son. Mum is greeted warmly by the 'welcomer' and handed a notice sheet. The boy is not acknowledged and is not given a notice sheet. As Jackie Cray says,

One is recognised, affirmed and involved; the other is often ignored, occasionally patronised and always kept firmly on the margin.

If we as adults went somewhere where we were constantly ignored, I suspect we would very soon cease to attend and yet our children, more often than not, have to endure this kind of situation week after week and then we are surprised when they don't want to go!

b. Patronising and embarrassing them.
Believe it or not, the majority of children are acutely embarrassed when 'on show'. For example, we may be surprised at the children's reluctance to be involved in 'silly' actions, while adults look on smiling, thinking (or worse still, saying) 'Oh, aren't they sweet!' Care must be taken to avoid putting children in this position.

Talking down to children can also have a patronising effect. We need to speak normally but use language that the children will easily understand.

3. By what we provide for them

a. Often accommodation for children's work is poor compared with that enjoyed by the adults. Equipment and furniture need to be 'child-friendly'.

b. Leaders who feel pressurised into volunteering out of guilt rather than calling.

c. Services/meetings that are adult orientated rather than those that are suitable for the whole family.

Our aim as Christians should be to live lives that are becoming more Christ-like. This needs to include our attitude towards children. The church should be a family where we honour and prefer one another (Romans 12:10). As Jackie Cray writes:

When Jesus founded his church he called everybody into a renewed experience of community. In the church we never stop being individuals, but if we are to be the community God intends us to be, we have to learn to let go of some of our twentieth-century individualistic attitudes.

The full potential of the church will only be realised when everybody has the attitude of 'I'm not here for me – I'm here for you'. Therefore, as adults, we may need to lay aside some of our preferences and seek to understand more fully the spiritual and practical needs of the children in our church family.

Exercise 1
List anything in your church that may cause children to feel excluded.

Exercise 2
What things can be done in your church situation to make children feel more included? What things could you personally do?

Children not adults

Children are not just mini-adults, nor are they just spiritual beings! They have different characteristics and therefore different needs. It is vital to have some understanding of how children 'tick' to be able to communicate effectively with them and create the right kind of environment in which they can meet God.

The basic characteristics of children can be divided into five main groups:

S: social

P: physical

I: intellectual

E: emotional

S: spiritual

These characteristics change as children get older and a child of 3 years will be very different when they are 10. Each child must also be seen as an individual, they are all different and these general characteristics will only provide a partial understanding. Children's leaders must make every effort to gain a good understanding of the individual children for whom they are responsible in order to effectively lead them.

Many of the characteristics listed below have both negative and positive sides to them. The job of children's leaders, together with the other adults that influence children's lives, is to bring out the positives and to enable children, with God's help, to deal with the negatives. A badly behaved child, or in other words, a child that exhibits non-conformist social behaviour, is often able to influence other children in a negative way; they often lead others into all kinds of trouble! A child like this may well have great leadership potential if only it can be turned around and used in a positive way, e.g. the most badly behaved child in your group may one day become the leader of your church – all things are possible with God!

SOCIAL

General social characteristics of 3-11 year olds are that they are non-conformist, talkative, instantaneous and persistent, and involvement is vital for them.

3-7s
Unselfconscious

Selfish/individualistic
Find large groups difficult
Copying is natural to them

7-11s
Selfconscious
Relate in groups/teams
Conscious of peers
Boys *v.* girls

PHYSICAL

Generally children from 3 to 11 years are very *energetic*!

3-7s
Uninhibited
Poor motor skills
Can't sit still!

7-11s
Motor skills developing
Co-ordination improving
Girls developing at different rate from boys

INTELLECTUAL

General intellectual characteristics for 3-11 year olds are that they are imaginative, they respond to the visual, their concentration spans are short (approximately one minute per year of their age), they have limited first-hand experiences, and are inquisitive.

3-7s
Interpret literally
Repetition is acceptable and necessary
Reading is non-existent or limited

7-11s
Reasoning and deductive skills are growing
Everything is boring!
Reading skills are improving

EMOTIONAL

General emotional characteristics of 3-11 year olds are that they are vulnerable and they respond more to those who are prepared to really 'give of themselves'.

3-7s
Long separations are bad news
Emotions are quickly aroused, can be deep but short-lived

7-11s
Becoming more independent
Emotionally more secure
More easily embarrassed
Selfconsciousness growing

SPIRITUAL

The spiritual characteristics of 3-11 year olds are basically the same throughout the whole of the time although the extent to which they are true does change. God is real to them, they can and do worship, they can and do hear God speak, they will pray, they will respond to God, they have implicit faith and they have limited language to explain their experiences.

Exercise 1
In what ways does a 4-year-old differ from a 10-year-old?

Exercise 2
What are the negative and positive aspects of the following characteristics?

For example, social characteristic – non-conformist. The negative is that children will want to do what they want to do rather than what you, as the leader, want them to do. The positive is that God wants children who are radically different from their non-Christian peers.

Talkative

Instantaneous

Persistent

The balanced programme

It is important that every programme is balanced but has lots of variety. Choose one point that you want to communicate and then select activities that will either teach this point or reinforce it. In addition to this, a programme should have some elements of praise, worship and prayer and opportunity for the children to respond to what God may have said to them. Also, a purely fun activity can be a valuable ingredient of any programme.

Bearing in mind the children's concentration spans, it is advisable to divide the programme running time into five- to ten-minute slots for 7-11 year olds. Then select items from the lists below to create your balanced programme.

Teaching
Bible story
Real life story
Object lesson
Drama
Puppets
Videos

Reinforcers
Activity sheet
Quiz/game
Memory verse
Small groups (for discussion/ministry)
Drama and puppets
Sword drill
Art and craft

Praise and worship
Singing
Praying
Dancing
Listening to God
Response/ministry

Fun
Games
Art/craft
Keep fit
Baking

Once you have chosen your 'ingredients', there are other factors to be borne in mind when ordering your programme.

1. Stand up/sit down?
Children need to change position at regular intervals (especially if sitting on the floor)

2. Listening/doing?
Children need active participation as well as just watching or listening.

3. Serious/fun?
Mix in the fun elements with the more serious ones.

To run a successful programme the following are of vital importance:

1. Thorough preparation, i.e. programme items, equipment, environment.

2. A strong leader/link person who will hold the meeting together.

3. No gaps between items – the programme needs to flow.

4. Good team work.

Below is an example of a possible one-hour programme for 7-11 year olds with the theme 'Be Strong and Courageous':

11:00 **Praise**. Choose two praise songs

11:05 **Teaching – Bible base Daniel 1**. Tell the story with visual aids.

11:15   **Memory verse – Joshua 1:9.** Use a game to gather the words (see section on Scripture verses).
      Song – 'Be Strong and Courageous' – from *Powerpack Praise.**

11:25   **Interactive Drama – 'Joshua'** – from *Play On Words.*†

11:35   **Puppets – 'Don't Be Afraid'** – from *Puppet Power.*†

11:40   **Worship/Prayer/Ministry** – Choose one or two worship songs and then give opportunity for the children to make a response, e.g. asking God to help them not be afraid/asking to be filled with the Holy Spirit/pray into areas of fear.

11:50   **Quiz** – Use quiz questions taken from the story.

11:58   **Prayer/Closing Song.**

* *Powerpack Praise* is available from the Powerpack Trust, 21A Mountside, Guildford, Surrey, GU2 5JD.

† *Play On Words* and *Puppet Power* are available from Kevin Mayhew Publishers.

Children's responses to God

Children can and do respond to God. There will always be some who may respond either to please the leader or because of peer pressure, but these are by far the minority. Children need to be given regular opportunity to respond to God in a variety of areas, e.g. salvation, healing, repentance, being filled with the Spirit, seeking gifts of the Spirit, etc.

CHILDREN AND SALVATION

1. The Gospel must be presented and explained in a way which is relevant to the age/social background and experience of the children (see below).

2. God's truths are spiritually discerned (1 Corinthians 2:12-14) and therefore the children will not necessarily have an intellectual understanding of all the elements of the Gospel.

3. Jesus said that children could believe in him (Matthew 18:6). The Greek word for believe here is the same as that used in Acts 16:31 in reference to the Philippian jailer. No one would doubt that the jailer had faith that led to his salvation but many have problems as to the validity of children's faith. In addition it is useful to note that the children in Matthew 16 are referred to as 'little ones' and the Greek word used is 'micros' from which we get our words like microphone and microscope, etc. It seems to imply that even little (young) children can believe and be 'saved'.

   Jesus added to this in Luke 10:21 when he said, 'I praise you, Father, Lord of heaven and earth, because you have hidden these things from the wise and learned, and revealed them to little children. Yes, Father, for this was your good pleasure.'

   D. L. Moody once said:

   You do not know how much infidelity there is in the church today with regard to child conversion. There are but a few who believe that children can become Christians; but thank God, there is a bright day coming.

   The above was written in the nineteenth century, the 'bright day' has taken a long time in coming!

4. It is impossible to say at what age a child can become a Christian.

   Charles Spurgeon said,

   A child of five, if properly instructed, can savingly believe as well as an adult. My conviction is that our converts from among children are among the best that we have. I should judge them to have been more numerously genuine than any other class, more constant, and in the long run, more solid.

   David Livingstone said,

   Our business is to teach children about sin and the Saviour, without even a hint about a certain age to accept Christ. The Holy Spirit will, in due time, convict them of sin. When he convicts of sin, whatever the age, who are we to dare to interfere with his work?

   Many well-known Christians have responded to the Gospel at a young age, e.g. Corrie Ten Boom at 5 years, Lord Shaftesbury at 8 years, Jonathan Edwards at 7 years and Isaac Watts at 9 years.

5. Children won't easily distinguish between making a commitment for the first time and re-commitment and so will often respond over and over again to become a Christian. It is necessary to help them understand that, while they only have to become a Christian once, there are other times when they might feel that, for instance, they haven't been doing very well as a Christian and they want to say sorry to God and make a new start. Sometimes children will keep responding because they haven't received any assurance of salvation, while others will just have difficulty understanding the language that the leader uses. Every time a child responds, however, it is vital that we encourage them and lead them to a place where they will be closer to God.

6. In these days when more and more children are growing up without a natural father or with negative experiences there is a tendency to shy away from presenting God as a Father. Obviously this is a very sensitive area but it

seems to me that children who don't have a natural father around need to know God as their Heavenly Father even more. However, it is vital that we ask God for wisdom and for sensitivity in approaching this.

OPTING IN OR OUT?

There are two main schools of belief as regards children and salvation.

1. All children start life in the Kingdom.
In other words all children are in the Kingdom until they opt out. Those that hold this position use Mark 10:13-16 as their key Scripture, where in verse 14 Jesus says, 'Let the little children come to me, for the kingdom of God belongs to such as these.' They believe that the 'such as these' is a reference to children.

Teaching children, when holding this belief, involves discipling and nurturing with the hope that they will not opt out.

2. All children start life outside the Kingdom.
This infers that children need to opt into the Kingdom. Scriptures such as Romans 3:23 where it says that 'all have sinned and fall short of the glory of God' are applied to children as well as to adults. Those that hold this view do recognise, however, that there is 'an age of accountability', before which a child is not held responsible for their sin.

In this case the job of children's leaders and parents is to present the gospel in such a way that children will want to opt in, in other words they have an evangelistic task.

N.B. Children who are brought up in a Christian home will often say that they have always loved Jesus. These children 'grow' into faith and may not be able to identify a particular time/day on which they made a 'decision' to become a Christian. If we are too 'decision orientated' the danger is that we will not accept the fact that such children are in the Kingdom. Our task should be to encourage these children to go deeper in faith rather than to ask them to start as a Christian.

PRAYING WITH A CHILD WHO WANTS TO BECOME A CHRISTIAN

1. Try and ascertain what they think a Christian is.

2. Ask them what has made them decide that they want to become a Christian.

3. Ensure that they are willing to admit that they have sinned. Encourage them to think of at least one thing that they have done which is sin and get them to say that they are sorry to God for it.

4. Encourage them to pray aloud, either using words of their own or words that you give them.

5. Pray for them to know that something has happened and for them to be filled with the Holy Spirit.

6. Be careful of the language that you use. For example, encouraging a child to ask Jesus into their heart won't be helpful when the child thinks in a literal way. I have heard of children who have wanted to know what food they should give to Jesus now that he is living inside them! Also don't have too high expectations of a child's ability to communicate about salvation. They may be responding to God speaking to them but not be able to explain what is happening – God works in their hearts and their heads need time to catch up!

7. Encourage children to tell somebody that they have become a Christian, if appropriate. Obviously it is good to encourage children to talk about what they have done but sensitivity in this area is vital. A child who comes from a non-Christian family may experience severe persecution and teasing if they race straight home after making a decision to become a Christian and tell their parents and siblings. They may not be strong enough to cope with this, so early on in their experience, and will consequently give up. In this kind of situation it would probably be better to encourage the child to share with another Christian and let them decide when they are ready to share with those who may not be overjoyed by the news. Don't ever tell a child not to share about their decision. We don't want them to be deliberately keeping secrets in this way; instead they need to be allowed to break the news in a natural way, in their own time, rather than because the person who led them to Christ says they have to.

8. Tell a child who becomes a Christian that this is just the beginning. God wants them to get

to know him more and more and for them to grow stronger and stronger as a Christian. Share with them some of the things that will help them grow, e.g. reading the Bible, prayer, fellowship, etc.

PRESENTING THE GOSPEL

In order to become a Christian a person, whether adult or child, will need to hear the Gospel. However, the danger is that we think that it is vital to have every theological 'i' dotted and 't' crossed before we can enter into a relationship with God. This, I believe, is not the case. To make an initial response and enter into salvation, it is sufficient to have a basic understanding of the fact that God loves us, even though we are sinners, and that he sent Jesus to die so that if we are really sorry (repent) we can be forgiven and enter into a relationship with him. (Children will need help to understand that sin isn't just robbing banks or murdering someone but taking a biscuit when mum has said they are not to have one before dinner, for example!)

A really simple but effective presentation of the Gospel is to use the wordless book that has been popular in children's evangelism for many, many years. It is based on the use of colours that represent different aspects of the Gospel.

The wordless book

Gold/yellow	God is the greatest, he made us, he loves us and he's in heaven (Exodus 15:12).
Dark/grey	We all do things that are wrong, the Bible calls this sin. As a result we are separated from God and it is like living in the dark (Romans 3:23).
Red	Jesus came to the earth and lived a perfect life. He took our punishment when he died on the cross. He rose again and now he is alive in heaven (1 Corinthians 15:3-4).
White	God wants us to be really sorry for our sin so that he can forgive us (1 John 1:9).
Blue	Baptism is a sign that our old life has gone and a new life has begun (2 Corinthians 5:17).
Green	We need to grow as Christians by praying, reading the Bible, meeting with other Christians and by

asking God's special helper, the Holy Spirit to lead and help us (John 14:26).

Sometimes the gold colour is used at the end rather than the beginning to talk about heaven. It is also possible to leave out the blue if your understanding of baptism is different.

I have made a worm out of circles of these colours, which is a little more appealing than an ordinary book. Cut out a circle from card (around 15cm in diameter – the size needs to reflect the size of the group with which it is going to be used) of each colour and if possible laminate them. Make two holes in the top, thread a length of string through them in the correct order. Stick some eyes on the gold circle and draw a mouth. Children can make their own worms out of coloured pompoms.

Alternatively make bracelets. Thread the appropriate colour beads on to some leather thonging (boys seem to be just as happy to wear them as girls are!). As well as a reminder of the Gospel it can also be a good witnessing tool.

Make a bookmark with the explanations above printed on it. Attach a short ribbon/cord to the bottom of the card on to which the beads can be threaded.

The above is just one way to present the Gospel but there are many others. Ask God to show you how best to present the Gospel to your children so that your presentation is age appropriate and takes into consideration their background, etc.

Children as well as adults need to accept Jesus as their Saviour and also allow him to be Lord of their lives but this may not all happen at one time. They need to be constantly challenged about how their relationship with God is and whether they are letting him be the 'boss'. Build response times on a regular basis into your meetings to give children frequent opportunities to take steps towards God.

Exercise 1

You want to share the Gospel with your group of children, how would you go about it? What sort of language and examples would you use?

Exercise 2

A child in your group says that they want to become a Christian. What would be your response? What questions would you ask, what would you do and what would you ask the child to do?

Wow! Look what God's done!
Children's testimonies

At first I was in a really dark place and I heard voices shouting at me. Then suddenly something grabbed my feet. It was dragging me backwards. *(He was literally crawling on the floor trying to get away.)* Then I saw a white person but the face was just bright lights. I grabbed for the hand that was held out by the person and then I knew that it was God. I went to heaven with him and saw people laughing and singing. I was so happy I had been saved by God. *(Leader – When he got up tears were streaming down his face and he said, 'I've seen God, I've seen God and he told me that he loved me!')*

Hadrian, aged 10

I had a picture of me in a cave. There was a scary man who was frightening children. I asked him why he didn't get me. He said there was a big man next to me and that it was an angel.

Emily, aged 8

Jesus came into my life and is growing things in me.

Tyler, aged 4

God gave me a big hug.

Katie, aged 5

God lifted a great weight off me, now I could do anything for God.

Sarah, aged 9

I had a really good time with my friends and God at Powerpack and I was really blessed by the things God did for me. On Tuesday I was prayed for because I felt really sad because my mum and dad have split up and God released the sadness inside me and filled me with happiness. On the same evening I went forward for prayer because some of the people in my class at school were unkind to me and I had no one to play with. I felt really sad and at Powerpack the sadness flowed out of me and I was able to enjoy the rest of the week.

On Friday, God told me that I will be a dancer. I can now speak in tongues without feeling embarrassed.

Michelle, aged 11

Last night I made God top of my list instead of TV and my friends.

Hannah, aged 9

When I got prayed for I was overloaded with the Holy Spirit.

Thanks, God; for the first time I've experienced your mighty power ministered to by a child of course!

Mike, 37!

God said that when I get older I'm going to be a Sunday school teacher.

Phil, aged 9

When I was getting filled with the Holy Spirit I saw myself standing in front of an angel and she had a big book and she ticked my name off and pointed to Jesus. I went up to him and I was bowing before his throne and I kissed his hand.

Jenny, aged 10

God filled me with the Holy Spirit and I got closer to him.

Hannah, aged 8

God used my friend and me to pray for someone and they got healed.

Emma and Leanne

God told me that I can make an impression on the world. I said, 'What do you mean?' God said, 'Each time you pray you help make an impression.' So I pray a lot for the world now.

Amber, aged 10

God has forgiven me for my sins. I feel filled with joy and happiness. I've never felt so clean inside before.

Catherine

Thank you, God, for giving me a new start absolutely free!

Sarah, aged 11

Children and the Holy Spirit

Jesus promised to send his Holy Spirit, the Helper (John 14:19) to the disciples because he knew that if they were to live in the way that he had shown them then they would need more than their own resources. Joel prophesied that God would pour out his Spirit on all people, young and old, male and female and yet so often children are not regarded as suitable candidates to receive the Spirit. Children need all the resources that God has for them if they are going to survive as Christians in what can often be a hostile world. The task of children's leaders and parents is to do all they can to facilitate children receiving from God all that they need to stand firm as Christians.

Children need the Holy Spirit

1. *To be a Christian*, to live according to God's laws, etc. (Romans 8:9 'If anyone does not have the Spirit of Christ, he does not belong to Christ').

2. *To benefit the church* (1 Corinthians 12:7 'Now to each one the manifestation of the Spirit is given for the common good').

3. *To enable them to worship* (John 4:23 'True worshippers will worship the Father in spirit and in truth').

4. *To give power for evangelism* (Acts 1:8 'But you will receive power when the Holy Spirit comes upon you, you will be my witnesses').

5. *To aid prayer* (Romans 8:26 'We do not know what we ought to pray but the Spirit himself intercedes for us').

There is no age restriction on being filled with the Holy Spirit, the only qualification is that the child is a Christian. Children often have far less problems than adults in this whole area because they don't try to understand or rationalise everything, they believe that God will give to them what he promises.

Children need to be given a balanced view of the Holy Spirit and his work.

WHO IS THE HOLY SPIRIT?

Even the words 'holy' and 'Spirit' can be fairly unintelligible to some children so it is important to make these clear. Children need to see that the Holy Spirit is God, part of the Trinity, a helper for them.

WHAT DOES THE HOLY SPIRIT DO?

A teaching series on people that help us can be a great way to look at the work of the Holy Spirit, for example:

Postman/mail man brings us letters/messages (the Holy Spirit brings messages from God to the people: 1 Corinthians 12:10b).

Teacher (the Holy Spirit is a teacher: John 14:26).

A policeman helps us keep the law (the Holy Spirit helps us keep God's law: John 16:13).

A dustman or refuse collector gets rid of our rubbish (the Holy Spirit convicts us of sin: John 16:8-9).

Doctors/nurses bring healing (one of the gifts of the Spirit is healing: 1 Corinthians 12:9b).

School crossing patrollers lead us in safety (Acts 16:7).

Parents care for us and give us encouragement (the Holy Spirit brings strengthening, encouragement and comfort: 1 Corinthians 14:3b).

This series can be reinforced by doing a craft project which involves making collage pictures of each of the above people with captions likening them to the Holy Spirit.

The Holy Spirit gives us supernatural gifts (1 Corinthians 12 and Romans 12).

Children will need teaching on what all these gifts are (word of knowledge, word of wisdom, faith, healing, miracles, prophecy, tongues, interpretation and discernment) and how to recognise them. Demonstration is one of the best teaching methods.

Children generally don't think that it is any 'big deal' to use the gifts of the Spirit, they take it all in their stride and it can seem quite clinical! We need to make it as easy as possible for them to enter into using the gifts, giving opportunity for them to share what they receive from God and taking them seriously. They will need practice in learning to listen to God and there should be times to do this built into our meetings.

Healing

The children will expect immediate results in the realm of healing and it is important not to squash their faith!

A girl suffering from really bad athlete's foot once asked me to pray for healing for her. I prayed (but honestly without a lot of faith). The girl, however, believed that God wanted to do this for her. I had moved on to pray for the next child when all of a sudden I heard a shriek from behind me. The girl had taken her shoes and socks off and the dressing on her foot and there was nothing there but normal skin; God had totally healed her.

However, it will also be necessary to think through how to help a child who prays for healing and there is no apparent change or who is prayed for without result. Generally speaking, children will be happy to keep praying or receiving prayer and they should be encouraged to persevere.

Visions/pictures

Children, even young ones, seem to find it easy to receive pictures from God and I learnt the valuable lesson, early in my ministry, that God knows just the best way to speak to children. A 5-year-old girl once came up to me during a time of worship saying that God had given her a 'picture'. To be honest I was a little sceptical but since she was very persistent I eventually gave her the microphone. She proceeded to share the following: 'A dog was running across a road and a car ran over it and squashed it.'

My heart sank and I was quickly thinking of what I should do to redeem the situation and regretting that I had given her the microphone. I turned to her in desperation and asked if she knew what God wanted to say through this picture. She proceeded to say that the car was like God and the dog was like Satan and God can squash Satan just like the car squashed the dog. It was a profound truth communicated in a simple, childlike way.

Children need to be given opportunity to receive from God and encouraged to share what he gives them but the leader should be prepared to comment on the pictures and to draw all the strands together.

If you sense that something which a child shares is not from God be very careful how you deal with it. Unless it is damaging or obviously anti-biblical just acknowledge it and move on. Too negative a response could cause the child not to contribute again. Where a child contributes something that is obviously from God emphasise that it is God speaking and encourage the children to respond.

The Holy Spirit produces fruit in our lives (Galatians 5:22-23).

There will need to be teaching about the fruit of the Spirit alongside encouraging the use of the gifts. However, it is important to remember that, although children might be confident in using the gifts, they will not suddenly become 'angels' overnight. Fruit takes time to grow! Be careful not to judge them too harshly, God still uses imperfect vessels.

PRAYING FOR CHILDREN TO BE FILLED WITH THE HOLY SPIRIT

1. Make sure that the child is a Christian.
2. Help them to feel as relaxed as possible.
3. Be careful about the language that you use.
4. If appropriate, talk to them about 'tongues', explaining for instance that they will actually have to open their mouths and speak out.
5. Tell them what you are going to pray and what you expect them to do.
6. Pray against fear and for courage to speak out as and when necessary.
7. Pray in English and then in tongues and encourage them to join in.
8. Be brief and simple.
9. Encourage children to pray for children but tell them how to pray.
10. Keep your eyes open and watch what the Spirit is doing.

DON'T FORGET THAT GOD IS MORE READY TO GIVE THAN WE ARE TO RECEIVE! Luke 11:11-13.

MANIFESTATIONS OF THE SPIRIT

Children need to be taught that, although they cannot see the Holy Spirit, they can sometimes see the effect that he has on people, like in Acts 2 on the day of Pentecost when the disciples were speaking in tongues and must have looked drunk since they received this accusation. Often when the Holy Spirit is at work and people see some manifestation, it acts as a visual aid of God being at work. Children, in my opinion, have greatly benefited from watching what happens to others when there has been some obvious manifestation. Sometimes they are even convinced that God is real and wants to do something in their lives because of the manifestations.

Practical tips

1. Don't ever suggest what might happen but instead be ready to give some explanation as and when there are any visible manifestations of the Spirit at work.

2. Keep emphasising that there is nothing to be afraid of. Both the children being touched by the Spirit, and those watching, may need some reassurance.

3. Tell children that they don't need to fake any manifestation. It is also vital that they are told that an outward manifestation does not make them any better a person than someone who doesn't experience any such manifestation.

4. If children experience any manifestation it is useful to talk with them afterwards encouraging them to share what God has done for them.

MINISTRY TIMES WITH CHILDREN

The biggest problem in any ministry time is what to do with the children who are not involved. Unfortunately they won't normally just sit and watch as adults will, nor do they have the option to leave as adults do. Having said this, however, sometimes when there is a strong sense of the presence of God, a quietness and stillness will affect all of the children.

Concentration spans need to be borne in mind even in ministry times, although God may override these!

It is good to be able to encourage the children to pray for one another but they will need some training in how to pray.

Try and make any ministry times as orderly as possible. I have sometimes taped lines on the floor and asked children to stand on them before they receive prayer.

KEYS TO GETTING STARTED

1. Ask God to raise our level, and the children's levels, of faith and expectation.

2. Ensure that the right environment is created, i.e. a good, balanced, fun-filled programme with space and time for God to work.

3. Do a comprehensive teaching series on the Holy Spirit.

4. Persevere.

OUR PART

1. Accept that this is an uncomfortable ministry where you have to rely totally on the Lord.

2. Remember that God is unpredictable and can be 'untidy'.

3. Let God be God, don't try and determine what he can and can't do.

4. Never expect a child to do something that you could not or would not do yourself!

5. Expect great things from God, he won't let you down. Have the attitude that says, 'I'm ready for anything, Lord.'

Exercise 1

Think about the language and examples that you would use to introduce the Holy Spirit and his work to the age group of child with which you work.

Exercise 2

Look at your current programme and think about where you could make some space for the Holy Spirit to work.

Children at risk!

In John 10:10 we are told that Satan's plan is to steal, kill and destroy, while God's is that we will have life and have it to the full. Our children are at risk from all sorts of things and situations. As children's leaders and parents it is vital that we do all that we can to protect them from coming to any physical, emotional or spiritual harm.

Children are at risk from obvious things like abuse but alongside this there are many subtle things that can have very negative effects on children. It is imperative that we identify these, make them known and if children have been involved in them, be able to deal with any consequences.

INTRODUCTION

Children of all ages are at risk through:

1. Violence

2. Abuse of all kinds

3. Dysfunctional families

4. Lack of discipline

5. Exposure to the media

6. School

7. Substance abuse, e.g. drugs, alcohol, etc.

8. Play (Many toys, computer games, etc., can have detrimental effects on children. Anything that becomes a craze needs to be looked at carefully.)

9. The attitude of the Church which can be exclusive rather than inclusive (See page 13.)

10. Not hearing the Gospel

CHILDREN: WHAT ARE THEY LIKE?

The minds of our children are open books ready for others to write their messages. Without careful and responsible guidance, those on whom our future rests will be harmed.

a. Their minds are like sponges, they believe what they hear, whether good or bad.

b. Their spiritual awareness/perception is high as regards both good and evil. Whatever is fed the most will be that which dominates the most!

c. They are imaginative. 'Let's pretend' is a popular fantasy. They can easily be drawn towards things with the potential for evil because they are by nature sinful.

d. They identify closely with fictional characters, so for instance children have tried to imitate characters like Superman, who can jump out of windows and fly through the air, with disastrous consequences! (The younger the child, the more difficult it is for them to distinguish between fact and fiction.)

e. They need clear boundaries/limits in all kinds of areas. 'My mum and dad say I can't' is sometimes easier to say than 'I don't want to!' when facing their peers.

f. Different children are affected and react in different ways to things that they see, hear or are involved in.

SO WHAT ARE WE FACING?

In 1989 the English Church census showed that 14 per cent of children under 15 were in a church-related activity on an ordinary Sunday. In 1998 it had decreased to 4 per cent whereas in the 1930s and 40s around 60 per cent of children were involved. (These statistics, however, may not give the whole picture, as for some children the equivalent of Sunday school is now a club that happens at another time in the week.)

On the other hand one in five children spends up to 30 hours a week playing video games and 13 per cent like specific games because of their violence. The world of our children is increasingly being controlled by the media, which portrays a more exciting world than the real one. Good and bad are mixed together in subtle ways that can lead to possible confusion, e.g. children's cartoons that seem harmless but have an underlying occult basis.

Traditionally, good versus evil was acceptable and the good always won. But now this is often not the case and when good does triumph, evil or violent methods are often used to gain the victory.

PROBLEM AREAS INCLUDE

1. TV
2. Videos and films
3. Computer games
4. Books
5. Toys
6. Games
7. Drugs/substance abuse
8. Advertisements
9. Music
10. Comics, magazines, newspapers

WHAT CAN WE DO ABOUT THIS?

Parents

1. Keep informed and advise children accordingly.

2. Offer good alternatives. This will require effort to find out what toys, TV programmes, etc., are good. Having done this, then spread the word to other parents.

3. Watch TV with their children. Help them discern the good and the bad.

4. Take an interest in their child's school.

5. Take children seriously. Ensure that they know what individual children can cope with, since children react to things in different ways.

6. Protect their child from premature exposure to adult values. Preserve fun and freedom of childhood in the home.

7. Take every opportunity to teach them the good, God's word, etc.

8. Have a good reason to explain why something is not good for them. It won't be good enough just to say 'no'. Be able to suggest appropriate alternatives.

9. Think carefully before allowing a child to have a TV in their bedroom, where they can watch all kinds of programmes that are not suitable for them.

10. Make being a Christian part and parcel of everyday life. Generate an atmosphere of faith, expectancy and excitement in the home.

11. Write and complain to TV producers, publishers, etc.

12. Make clear boundaries. Be consistent.

13. Don't be paranoid! Be balanced.

THE ROLE OF THE CHURCH

To provide a backup support system . . .

for parents:

1. Training – prevention is much better than cure.

2. Keep them informed. It can be very useful for the children's ministry department in a church to appoint someone who will do some research as to what are the current TV programmes, computer games, videos, toys, etc. Recommendations (not legislation) can then be made to parents about the suitability of them and also a list can be drawn up of things that are OK.

3. Counselling – helping them to know how to pray for their children.

4. Prayer for them to have wisdom in dealing with their children.

for children:

1. Recognise their value and spiritual potential.

2. Ensure that children's meetings are exciting, spiritual, relevant.

3. Teach children what's right and wrong. 'It is better to educate children than . . . repair adults' (Bill Wilson).

4. Provide counselling.

5. Prayer.

6. Evangelism

CONCLUSION

A child was once asked what he wanted to be when he grew up. He said a gangster or a Christian. It depends on who gets me first! As Christians we have an enormous responsibility.

What begins with the kindly and gentle wizard of pre-school storytelling who casts his helpful spells to aid the unfortunate, can have its end in something considerably less cosy. Cute and cuddly lion cubs grow up into full-grown lions. Parents beware! (Andrew Boyd)

Exercise 1

Go to the local library or bookshop and make a list of books that children should avoid and a list of books that will be helpful to them.

Exercise 2

Watch children's TV and list those programmes that are good for children to watch.

Section 2

Art and craft

On the whole most children enjoy creative work – especially art and craft. The need to experiment and discover, and the sense of achievement is all very important to them. They enjoy learning new skills, and working with various materials can be fun! The 'art and craft' session can also be a time when children develop socially as a group, as they share materials, exchange ideas and help one another. The activity can also be a relevant and fun way of reinforcing the teaching and gives leaders the opportunity to relate to the children individually rather than as a group.

Most of the art and craft projects we do are individual, i.e. each child produces a piece of work and then is eager to take it home! (This is especially true for younger children.) However, from time to time it is good to initiate group projects. The children then work together to produce something that can be used to enhance and decorate their meeting room or some other part of the church. It is vitally important to create an inviting environment for children's meetings wherever possible. So often church rooms are really quite bare with maybe a few 'bits and pieces' of children's work hastily stuck up on the wall – comparing very unfavourably with school.

Singing a few songs, telling a Bible story, having a quiz and finishing with some craft work has been the tradition in many of our church Sunday Schools over the years. Robbie Castleman in his book, *Parenting in the Pew* (IVP, 1993), writes:

> *Too many children's churches are 'cut-and-paste' times to keep children occupied until the adult service is over.*

So before planning an art and craft activity perhaps we should ask ourselves the following questions:

1. Why are we doing this? Is it a reinforcer? Is it so that we can cover up a bare wall? (Which can be a good idea!) Is it just for fun or a time-filler?

2. Is the project a possibility? Try one for yourself first to discover any problems and have an example to show the children where possible.

3. Is it relevant and/or suitable for the age group involved? Is it poor quality? Will it prove boring or frustrating or give a sense of achievement?

4. What are the capabilities of the children? Concentration spans? How much will you need to do beforehand, i.e. cutting out, etc.? Motor skills? How well will they share? How interested are they in detail?

5. Am I well prepared? Discipline problems can arise if not! Think ahead and have everything ready to hand. What will you do with the children who finish early? Will you need water for washing hands and a towel? Will you need extra helpers?

6. Is your equipment in good order? Sharp scissors? Felt tips that work? Suitable glue?

Not everyone will have the creative gifts to be able to initiate and organise an art and craft activity and therefore this may be a good opportunity to involve other church members who have those ideas and skills and would be willing to help on a one-off basis.

ART AND CRAFT IDEAS

Below are just a few ideas for art and craft. Keep an eye out for books of craft ideas especially at car boot or jumble sales.

Paint: Free painting
          Blow painting
          Printing – potato/various shapes and textures/sponge/hands and feet!
          Stencilling

Collage: Make pictures either individually or working as a group using various materials, e.g. fabric, tissue paper, sticky paper, cotton wool, sequins, coloured magazine pages, pasta, buttons, sand, sawdust, string, etc. (Painting a background first can be effective if a group project.)

Craft: Banners – large or small
           Masks
           Box-modelling
           Fimo
           Clay
           Salt dough
           Stone painting
           Origami
           T-shirt painting
           Shell models
           Teasel figures
           Musical instruments
           Puppets
           Binca
           Table decorations
           Calendars
           Cards
           Bookmarks
           Bead work
           Painting with glass paint onto acetate

Cooking: Sweet making
           Biscuit-making, cakes, gingerbread men,
           Rice crispy cakes, etc.
           Simple lemon drink
           Pizza
           Toffee apples

Children and mission

Children today are more aware of world events, etc., than ever before. Extensive news coverage of happenings around the world, all the information that is available via the Internet and increased opportunities for travel have all made the world seem like quite a small place. This needs to be used to advantage in order to encourage children to develop an interest in missions.

When asked what a missionary is, most children will say that it is someone who builds churches or stands in front of people telling them about Jesus. Of course this is what a missionary is in its purest sense, but today mission usually includes far more. In fact many countries would refuse admission to someone calling themselves a missionary but would be happy to welcome them as an engineer, doctor, teacher, etc. There is also almost an unspoken view that anyone who is a 'missionary' is a special person and a 'super' Christian. Children, as well as many adults, need to have their view broadened to see that missionaries are just ordinary people who have responded to God's call and are letting him use their skills and gifts wherever he wants to.

ENCOURAGING AN INTEREST IN OVERSEAS MISSION

1. Put a world map on the wall where your children's group meets. Encourage children to get a similar map to put on their bedroom wall at home.

2. Read stories about missionaries to the children and encourage them to do the same. There are a number of books containing missionary stories that have been written specifically for children, e.g. *The TrailBlazers* series published by Christian Focus Publications.

3. Encourage the children to get on a mailing list to receive magazines that have a missionary

focus, e.g. Tear Fund, the Baptist Missionary Society's WOW club.

4. As a children's group or a family, sponsor a child in another country.

5. Organise an activity to raise money for a particular project.

6. If the church supports a missionary, write letters or emails, or make an audio or videotape to send.

INVOLVEMENT IN OVERSEAS MISSION

There are two main areas in which children can get involved:

1. Intercession

Children need to understand that intercession is basically 'standing in the gap' for people and situations.

Practical ideas to involve children in intercession for mission

1. Possibly the best place to start is to encourage them to pray for any missionaries from their own church. There is then the possibility that, when these missionaries come home for a visit, the children can hear first-hand details about the work that they are doing.

2. Focus on the story of someone who is doing some significant work for God now, e.g. Jackie Pullinger, Bill Wilson (working in Brooklyn, USA, where his team are reaching approximately 20,000 children a week with the gospel), etc. It is particularly good to focus on people or organisations that are working with children or young people so as to make it easier for children to relate, e.g. The Toybox Charity which is working with street children in Guatemala (PO Box 660, Amersham, Bucks, HP6 6EA. (Tel. 01494 432591)

3. Use the prayer tools that Esther Network International produce (854 Conniston Road, West Palm Beach, Florida 33405-2131, USA. Tel. 407-832-6490. Fax. 407-832-8043). (See details in the Prayer Activities section.)

4. Use an event taking place in a certain country to form a focus for prayer, e.g. Chinese New

Year (Jan/Feb). Combine it with art and craft activities by making something Chinese, e.g. a Chinese lantern or kite or maybe eat some Chinese food together, etc.

5. Write to missionary organisations which produce materials for children (see list of addresses below). Some of them, like the Baptist Missionary Society and Tear Fund, also include lots of ideas for working with children's groups. WEC also loan ethnic costumes, artifacts, music, pictures and posters, etc., which can create lots of interest.

6. Construct a board game based on a world map with 'prayer squares'. When a player takes a card, that individual or the group prays for whatever is written on the card (the cards should be updated regularly). Other squares could have things like 'struck down with malaria, stay in hammock for a week – miss a turn', etc.

7. Start a Daniel Prayer Group. Contact YWAM who have initiated these. Their stated purpose for such groups is 'to lead children, teens and families world-wide into a deeper friendship with God and to pray for world revival and the completion of world evangelisation'.

8. Find some pictures of children from different countries, talk about them and then encourage children to pray. The book *Children Just Like Me,* published by Dorling Kindersley, is a good source of pictures, as is the internet.

9. Use books like *You can change the world* and *You too can change the world* (available from WEC), which give information and prayer topics for various countries and people groups. WEC also produce a large range of information/activity packs for children.

10. Encourage the children to get a pen friend. Children in other countries, e.g. Romania, who are learning English, are keen to correspond with a person who speaks English as their first language.

Contact Chime Worldwide (see list of addresses below) who publish a very helpful catalogue of mission materials for children and also have a Stopwatch Club for children to join.

2. Short-term mission programmes

There are not many opportunities for the under-11s to actually go on a short-term mission. Perhaps if a church team goes out to visit a missionary situation they could consider taking a child. This can be an extremely valuable experience for the child and God may well choose to use a child in preference to an adult in some situations.

King's Kids. This is the children's wing of YWAM and they offer mission opportunities both in this country and overseas for children from 8 years and up.

CONCLUSION

It is a fact that the majority of people who are on the mission field today were called by God when they were children. It is therefore very important that children, from an early age, are exposed to the possibility that God might want to use them overseas.

Of course it is also important that mission and evangelism are not just presented as things that happen overseas. God will want children to be missionaries (ambassadors for him) in their school and in their own local areas.

USEFUL ADDRESSES

ARAB WORLD MINISTRIES
PO Box 51
Loughborough
Leicestershire
LE11 OXQ

BAPTIST MISSIONARY SOCIETY
PO Box 49
Didcot
Oxon
OX11 8XA

CHIME WORLDWIDE
11a Upper Teddington Road
Kingston upon Thames
Surrey
KT1 4DL

LEPROSY MISSION
Goldhay Way
Orton Goldhay
Peterborough
Cambs
PE2 OGZ

OVERSEAS MISSIONARY FELLOWSHIP
Belmont
The Vine
Sevenoaks
Kent
TN13 3TZ

TEAR FUND
100 Church Road
Teddington
Middlesex
TW11 8QE

WEC INTERNATIONAL
Bulstrode
Gerrards Cross
Bucks
SL9 8SZ

WYCLIFFE BIBLE TRANSLATORS
Horsleys Green
High Wycombe
Bucks
HP14 3XL

YWAM
King's Kids
Stanley House
Stanley Crescent
Paisley
PA2 9LF

Exercise 1

Write to some of the missionary societies listed in this section and ask for details of children's materials that they produce. Start making a collection of resources.

Exercise 2

Read some missionary stories for yourself and summarise one or two that are suitable to tell the children. Ask someone in the church who is good at drawing to illustrate them for you. (Black-and-white line drawings are the best since these can be photocopied onto OHP sheets and then coloured.)

Children and the Bible

All Scripture is God-breathed and is useful for teaching, rebuking, correcting and training in righteousness. (2 Timothy 3:16)

The Bible should be the basis for all that we do amongst children. One of the greatest aims of any children's leader should be to introduce children to the Bible in such a way that they learn what is in it. Even more important is that they come to see it as the word of God and therefore the instruction book upon which their life needs to be built. They need to be told that God's word and the Scriptures are alternative names for the Bible – don't assume that they will know!

It seems that it has always been hard to involve children in Bible reading as evidenced by this quotation from *The Good Seed* by J. C. Pollock and reproduced by Terry Clutterham in his book *The Adventure Begins*:

In 1877 a girl of eighteen or twenty, Annie Marston . . . went to live with the family of Canon Harsford-Battersby, who a few years earlier had founded the Keswick Convention. She took a class of small girls in the Sunday School, and encouraged them to read the Bible on their own during the week, with little success. 'I have tried, over and over again,' one child would say, 'but I could never keep on! There were such long lists of names, I couldn't even read them, so I gave up' . . . 'I got to such difficult chapters, I couldn't understand them, so I gave up.' Miss Marston wrote out weekly for each child 'a list of portions to read daily until the following Sunday, on the understanding that during morning school we would talk about difficult parts, and that they might ask questions freely. Very soon they became so eager, and their questions were so many and sometimes so important, though their ages were mainly from eight to ten, that it was impossible to get through in the limited time at our disposal.'

Things haven't changed much since that time. Although there are more Bibles sold in a year than any other book and there are many more Bible reading aids than ever before, statistics from a small survey of children showed a serious problem. I gave 118 children from seven different churches a questionnaire to complete. The children were aged between 6 and 13 and were almost exclusively from Christian families. Of the 118 only 17 said that they read the Bible every day and of these 16 used Bible reading notes of some kind. Another 21 said that they read on quite a lot of days while 77 admitted to only reading every now and then. 39 read with a parent, 50 in their church groups and only 17 with their family. The Good News Bible proved to be the most popular followed closely by the International Children's Bible.

These statistics show a sad state of affairs. Children for the most part are just not getting into the Bible on any regular basis despite the fact that 90 per cent said that they liked reading books. They obviously need a lot of help to be able to access, what to them, is a very large book and one which does not look at all child-friendly.

Why is this the case?

1. Reading abilities are lower.

2. People don't see the relevance of the Bible; children have an even harder time as they are bombarded with so much negative criticism.

3. This is the age of the computer!

4. It takes effort and discipline to really get into the Bible, but our society is one that wants things without these. If you don't gain quickly and easily from something, then why do it?

What's the answer?

1. Children (and adults for that matter) need to be given a good reason why they should read the Bible. They need to be convinced that it is not just another book but that it is the book that God gave to us because he loves us and wants us to have the best life possible – a life spent in relationship with him and each other. He tells us how to have this in the Bible. Reading the Bible should not just be about learning the facts but also discerning God's voice and applying the truths it contains to our everyday lives.

2. It will be necessary to make the Bible as 'child-friendly' as possible. Children need to be given 'bite-size' pieces – the whole will be too much for even the most proficient readers.

3. Variety is the spice of life, a fact that is truer in this day and age than ever. It is imperative to present the Bible to children in our churches and homes in a variety of different ways. Yesterday's ways are often like 'stale bread' to the children while they are crying out for 'fresh' bread. Also, in the area of Bible reading they will need to be introduced to different methods, different notes, etc. It is also important to remember that children learn in different ways and it will be necessary to discover the different learning styles of our children in order to best meet their needs.

4. Children who have experienced God by his Spirit and have been used by God in hearing and speaking his word need constant encouragement to continue in this. However, they also need to have emphasised to them that this is only part of the picture. Hearing from God through the written word is just as important and in fact the Bible must be the ultimate authority to judge any prophetic words.

5. Children's leaders and parents need to be good 'role models' in this area of the Bible. If the leader or parent is someone who 'loves' the Bible and who places great importance on it, then there is every likelihood that the children in that person's group will follow suit. Share examples of how God has spoken to you through the Bible and what a difference it has made in your life. Also share testimonies of how important the Bible has been in people's lives, e.g. in countries where Christians are persecuted, the story of Mary Jones, etc.

6. Use computers more in both learning and reading situations. I can't prove this but my suspicion is that interactive Bible reading activities on the computer would be a much more attractive option to many children than sitting down with an actual Bible and a book of Bible reading notes!

7. Children will need to be given some understanding of the background of the Bible, the fact that it is about specific people who lived at specific times in history. Also, although people were actually responsible for writing the different books from which it is made up, they were only actually writing as God inspired them. It is not a fictional make-believe story like the other things that children may read, but the inspired word of God.

8. I believe that the aim of children's leaders, in conjunction with parents (if they are Christians), should be to encourage children to develop a 'habit' of daily Bible reading/study. The earlier this is done in a child's life the better. If they start from an early age knowing that they should spend time with the Lord (which should include worship, prayer and Bible reading), then hopefully it will stay with them throughout their lives. However, if this becomes just an intellectual exercise rather than a time when the living God speaks to the child straight from his word, they will soon lose interest. They need help to learn how to connect regularly with God as they read his word. There is also a need to be realistic; some days they just won't make it and they will need help to cope with the feelings of condemnation and failure that often come at times like these.

Children need to

1. Learn to find their way around the Bible. (Encourage the children to use the Contents page to help them find what they are looking for, engage in activities which will help them with this. See the Bible Activities, page 40, for ideas).

2. Learn what it actually says (many children from non-Christian homes are totally ignorant of what would be regarded as the most famous stories of the Bible). It is also important to use a modern version of the Bible that is appropriate to their age, e.g. The New International Children's Bible for 6-12 years.

3. Learn how to apply the truths that it contains, to their everyday lives.

Patricia W. Van Ness says in her book, *Transforming Bible Study with Children* (Abingdon Press, 1991):

As long as the gospel and indeed the whole Biblical story, remains a 'head trip', only an intellectual exercise – it cannot be transforming. It is only when it becomes a part of your whole being – mind, body, emotions, spirit and community, that it changes the way you perceive, feel and respond.

4. Learn how to meditate on it and to use it as a vocabulary for prayer.

5. Memorise verses which they can recall at times when they need them.

6. Learn how to use it as the 'sword' of the Spirit, particularly when under spiritual attack.

Our task as children's leaders and parents is not going to be an easy one but it is imperative that we do all we can to help children develop a love for the Bible and a desire to meet with God every time they read it. We need to be asking God the creator to gift us with ideas and plans that will help us in this task.

Exercise 1

Make a list of ways in which God has spoken to you from the Bible. Which of these could you share with your children?

Exercise 2

Choose some verses which could be used to 'feed on' in different situations.

Bible reading calendar

There are verses to look up in the Bible for 28 days.
Fill in the missing words and colour the numbered
Bibles as you do them.

1 Jesus is the _ _ _ _ _ _ of God **John 1:29**	**2** Jesus is the _ _ _ _ of God **John 1:49**	**3** Jesus turned water into _ _ _ _ **John 2:1-10**	**4** Jesus said that a person must be _ _ _ _ again **John 3:3**	**5** God loved the _ _ _ _ _ so much he sent Jesus **John 3:16**	**6** If you believe in him you will have _ _ _ _ **John 3:16**	**7** Jesus is the _ _ _ _ _ of life **John 6:35**
8 Jesus is the _ _ _ _ _ of the world **John 8:12**	**9** Jesus is the _ _ _ _ for the sheep **John 10:7**	**10** Jesus came to give us _ _ _ _ **John 10:10**	**11** Jesus is the good _ _ _ _ _ _ _ _ **John 10:11**	**12** Jesus is the _ _ _ _ _ _ _ _ _ _ **John 11:25**	**13** Jesus raised _ _ _ _ _ _ _ to life **John 11:38**	**14** The people waved _ _ _ _ branches **John 12:13**
15 We should _ _ _ _ one another **John 13:34**	**16** Jesus said that he would _ _ _ _ back **John 14:3**	**17** Jesus said, 'I am the _ _ _ _' **John 14:6**	**18** Jesus said, 'I am the _ _ _ _ _', **John 14:6**	**19** Jesus said, 'I am the _ _ _ _', **John14:6**	**20** Jesus said he would give _ _ _ _ _ **John14:27**	**21** Jesus is the _ _ _ _ **John 15:5**
22 Eternal life is knowing _ _ _ **John 17:3**	**23** _ _ _ _ _ said that he did not know Jesus **John 18:15-18**	**24** Pilate said Jesus was _ _ _ _ of the Jews **John 18:33**	**25** Thomas said, 'My _ _ _ _ and my _ _ _', **John 20:28**	**26** Jesus asked _ _ _ _ _ if he loved him **John 21:15**	**27** Peter said that Jesus knew _ _ _ _ _ _ _ _ _ **John 21:17**	**28** Jesus did _ _ _ _ other things **John 21:25**

Bible activities

The apostle Paul said that it was necessary for us to be all things to all men in order that we reach people with the Gospel. I believe that this principle should be applied to all that we do with children and will stand us in good stead as we consider how we can best encourage children to get into the Bible. We need God's ideas and the ability to see things from the children's point of view if we are going to succeed. Below are some of the things that I have tried over the years. The list is by no means exhaustive but represents things that I have found successful with the children with whom I have worked.

ENCOURAGING CHILDREN TO READ THE BIBLE FOR THEMSELVES

My survey showed that the children who read the Bible every day were those that used some kind of Bible reading notes, so if we can encourage the use of notes it may well help the children to develop a habit of regular Bible reading. Children are all very different, however, so the more options that they can be given, the more likely it will be that we will hit on something that 'works' for them. It is probably important to 'ring the changes' as well so that they don't get bored. The more this involves parents the more success there will be.

1. Encourage the use of Bible reading notes such as those produced by Scripture Union, CWR and Powerpack, Time Out notes, etc.

2. Produce a weekly/monthly sheet with suggested daily Bible readings and a range of different activities, e.g.

   a. Bible readings and pictures to colour.

   b. Bible readings and puzzles to do.

   c. Bible readings and questions to answer of a purely factual nature.

   d. Bible readings and questions to answer involving the children in thinking about how the verses apply to their lives.

   e. A calendar highlighting one verse to read each day and a word to fill in. (See example with verses from John's Gospel on page 39. Other examples are included in the pack 'Training Up Children of the Word', produced by Powerpack.)

Encourage the children to do these during the week and then to bring them back to talk about in their groups the following week.

Points to bear in mind when preparing these kinds of sheets:

The Bible passage selected should not be too long.

The age and reading ability of the children need to be considered.

The sheets need to look attractive and inviting and need to be well produced.

FINDING THE WAY ROUND THE BIBLE

The Bible is a big book to cope with even as an adult; imagine what it is like to a child with limited reading ability. Never be afraid to encourage children to use the Contents page to find a specific book and do some teaching with the children about chapters and verses – what is obvious to us may not be to them!

Other activities could include:

Sword drill

This is a game to help children find their way around the Bible. Decide which verses you want the children to find and then give the children the following instructions:

1. Put your Bible under one arm (pretending that it is a sword in its sheath).

2. Find . . . (Give the children the reference of the first verse you want them to find).

3. 'Draw your swords' (The children take the Bible from under their arms and hold it in the air).

4. 'Charge' (The children have to find the verse as quickly as they can).

The first child to find it can be asked to read aloud, but be prepared to help them. Often if you have three or four turns, the same child will be the winner each time, so be creative about who you ask to read – maybe choose the second one, etc. It is important to know the reading abilities of those in a particular group since it is extremely important that a child is never put in a position of being asked to read something of which they are not capable.

Bible library

Collect 66 matchboxes or something similar. Cover them with coloured paper, e.g. green for Genesis to Deuteronomy (the books of Moses), blue for the prophets, Isaiah to Malachi, red for the Gospels, etc. Make a bookcase out of strong cardboard and put the 'books' in the correct order on the shelves. Encourage the children to learn the order a few at a time; build the learning process into a game or competition.

Bible steps

Write each of the names of the books of the Bible on a small card. Each child selects one card from the pile (without looking) and goes to one end of the room, making a line across it. Designate a finishing line (which probably needs to be the equivalent of 6-8 steps from the start). The leader calls out a letter from the alphabet and any child whose Bible book name contains that letter takes one step forward. Continue this until the first child reaches the finishing line or has all their letters called, they are then the winner. (If a name contains more than one of a particular letter then the appropriate number of steps is taken, for instance Ecclesiastes contains three 'E's so three steps would be taken). Decide how many times you are going to play, keep account of the winners of each game, totalling them to find an overall winner.

A variation of the above, when there is a lack of space, could be that instead of taking steps, the children could take a counter or something similar and total these.

Pile-up

Divide the children into two groups. Gather together as many Bibles as you can and make a pile, one for each group. Choose a verse that the children have to find in each of the Bibles in the pile. The winning group is the one to have all the Bibles in their pile open at the same place in the quickest time. Do this a few times and keep score so that you get an overall winner.

Bible relay

Divide the children into two teams. Each team needs a set of 66 cards with a book of the Bible written on each. One child in each team needs a Bible to refer to. Put the two sets of cards in separate boxes at one end of the room. A member of each team runs from the other end of the room and collects the card with Genesis on and then brings it back to the starting place. The next person runs and finds the card with Exodus on and so on until all 66 cards have been collected and laid out in the correct order. An alternative would be to get two sets of 66 Duplo bricks and label each with a book of the Bible. The children collect them and build a tower with the bricks/ books in the correct order.

GROUP READING ACTIVITIES

I believe that it is important to encourage children to bring their Bibles with them to meetings. It is equally important to use them once they bring them! It may not be appropriate to read a Bible passage together every time you meet but on occasions it is a good thing to do. Don't read around the group one verse at a time because this puts pressure on children who don't read very well but also breaks up the passage too much, making it difficult for children to follow. Below are some suggestions as to how to make group Bible reading more interesting:

Dramatic reading

Read the passage as a drama. Somebody will need to read the part of the narrator, others the characters in the story and everyone can read group parts. This could be further developed so that the children act as it is read. More understanding is needed to act than just read because it is necessary to start thinking and feeling, as characters would have done at the time. A further development of this could be to videotape the drama.

Modelling

Read the passage to the children while they follow in their own Bibles (much easier if they have the same version). Then give each of them a piece of clay or play dough and ask them to make something that sums up the passage for them as the leader reads it again. Look at the models and discuss why they made what they did.

Movement/Mime

Similar to above but, instead of modelling something from clay, encourage the children to put some movement/mime to the Bible passage. Have flags and ribbons available. If you can have some music playing in the background while you are reading, all the better. (Ecclesiastes 3:1-8 is a good passage to use for this.)

Reading the Psalms antiphonally

Hebrew poetry, such as the Psalms, was not written verse by verse but phrase by phrase. So for example Psalm 139 would read as follows:

1. Lord, you have examined me.

2. You know all about me.

1. You know when I sit down and when I get up.

2. You know my thoughts before I think them.

Divide the children into two groups or choose two individuals to read in this way.

Where would I fit?

Read the Bible passage together and then as the leader reads it a second time get the children to think about where they would fit in the story. For example, in the story of the Good Samaritan who would they have been like? Give them paper and felt pens or crayons and ask them to draw a picture as you read.

Cartoons

Ask the children to draw cartoons of the passage as it is read. It would probably help the children if you decide how many frames you expect beforehand and provide them with a piece of paper with the correct number of boxes marked out.

GENERAL ACTIVITIES

1. Make bookmarks with Bible verses on them, e.g. make a light bulb one with 'I am the light of the world' on it.

2. Make a mobile of the things that the Bible is like, e.g. lamp, hammer, honey, milk, sword, mirror, bread, etc.

3. Make a command/promise module. Use the simple origami activity to make a 'chooser' out of a square piece of paper with Bible commands, promises, etc.

4. Make a promise box to encourage the children to focus on the many promises of God in the Bible. Each child needs to make a small box or

to cover one that they already have. Construct sheets of 'promise cards', for each child and either pre-cut them or allow the children to cut them (depending on the age and ability of the group). The children can decorate the cards and then put them in their promise box. They then need to be encouraged to regularly take a card out and read it, thereby reminding them of God's promises. After a while prepare another sheet with different promises.

5. Select about six verses and write each one on a separate piece of paper. Stick them on the wall around the room. Give an example of an everyday situation that the children might face and tell them to go and stand by the verse that might help them or that they need to remember in that particular situation. This could lead into discussion as to why they chose a particular verse and how to 'feed' on it, e.g. a child's family is going to move to another city and they don't want to go, would link with Jeremiah 29:11: 'For I know the plans I have for you', declares the Lord, 'plans to prosper you and not to harm you, plans to give you hope and a future.' Perhaps a member of the child's family is very ill and is in hospital would link with Philippians 4:6-7: 'Do not worry about anything. But pray and ask God for everything you need. And when you pray always give thanks. And God's peace will keep your hearts and minds in Christ Jesus.'

6. Bible posters: Encourage the children to design a poster from 'scratch' or give them a pre-designed one that they can decorate. Put a verse or passage from the Bible on it and encourage them to think it as they are working on it. Use computer-generated borders and clip art.

7. All together dramas: These are a fun way of teaching children Bible stories. An example is included in the section on Drama on page 64, and more can be found in the Powerpack book *Play on Words* (published by Kevin Mayhew).

THE BIBLE IN WORSHIP AND PRAYER

Encourage children to come with a passage of Scripture to read as part of the worship.

Pray God's word. Choose a verse of Scripture for each child. Get them to think about it and use it as a basis for a prayer, e.g. Psalm 23:1: 'The Lord is my Shepherd, I shall lack nothing.' A possible prayer could be something along the lines of 'Father, thank you that you look after me and give me everything I need.'

Children and the prophetic

INTRODUCTION

A prophet is someone who hears from God and communicates his message to people. The Greek word for 'prophesy' implies 'to speak for another'. There are two parts to this, firstly a person has to 'hear' God say something, and then, secondly, they have to communicate what is heard. Children will need practice in both of these areas.

Prophecy, then, is a specific word from God, for a particular congregation or individual, delivered by a particular person at a particular time. More often than not, this is communicated verbally as a statement or described as a picture or vision. However, it would seem in these days that God is inspiring alternative ways of communication in the form of prophetic action, drama, dance, art, music and so on. This is nothing new – the Bible is full of the enactment of prophecy and symbolic acts; for example,

a. Ezekiel was told to pack up all his belongings and dig through a wall, taking them with him as a sign of the coming exile (Ezekiel 12:1-11).

b. Hosea was told by God to marry a prostitute (Hosea 1).

c. Jeremiah was told to buy a linen belt and to bury it. When it was dug up, it was ruined and it was to be a sign that the Lord was going to ruin the pride of the Israelites (Jeremiah 13:1-11).

Other examples can be found in Jeremiah 13:1-5; 18:1ff; Isaiah 20:1ff; Ezekiel 4:1ff; 5:1ff, and Acts 21:10-11.

CHILDREN AND THE PROPHETIC

Children, once they have been taught something of the ways in which God speaks, seem to find it easy to hear him. In the context of a meeting, it is important to have a specific time of quiet when they are encouraged to listen. Children respond to the visual, and God, knowing this, often seems to speak to them in picture form. More often than not, a child to whom God has given a picture is encouraged to either share it verbally or to write it down. It would probably be much easier for them if they could either draw the picture or, in some cases, act out what they have seen.

A useful introduction to these forms of sharing God's word is workshops which start with encouragement to draw/act/dance, etc., certain moods, emotions, situations, or truths, before actually going on to ask God to speak.

Prophetic art workshop
Equipment
pieces of paper as large as table space allows
paint or large felt-tip pens

Introductory activities
1. Choose two very different pieces of music and get the children to draw whatever the music makes them think about (abstract or concrete) as they listen.

2. Choose a worship song and do the same as above.

3. Read a passage of Scripture (e.g. Revelation 22:1-2) and ask them to draw something to portray it.

4. Ask them to draw a picture of what it is like to be filled with the Holy Spirit, for example.

Hearing from God
Pray and ask God to speak. Encourage the children to draw what he shows them. (It may still be necessary for them to verbally explain but at least they will have their 'picture' to help them.)

Prophetic movement/action
Equipment
ribbons, flags, sticks, etc.

Introductory activities
1. Act out/express different emotions, e.g. anger, joy, love, fear . . .

2. Express general truths, e.g. God loves you, love one another, God has set us free, God has given us power, God forgives, etc.

3. Read a passage of Scripture, e.g. Ecclesiastes 3:1-8 and act/dance it.

Hearing from God
Pray and ask God to speak. Encourage the children to act out/dance what he says to them.

CONCLUSION

It is important to encourage creativity in the children as they to listen to God. Give them opportunity to express what he says in their own way – this may be using one or more of the above forms.

Exercise 1
Make a list of ways in which God has spoken to you through prophetic words that you can share as examples with the children.

Exercise 2
Prepare a presentation based on the occasions in the Bible when God told people to do unusual things as prophetic actions.

Creative teaching

SPIRITUAL TEACHING

Spiritual teaching, in its simplest form, is taking a spiritual truth and communicating it in such a way that it will be understood, received and applied to the lives of those hearing. We teach in a variety of ways, some direct, e.g. with words, and others indirect, e.g. through actions and example.

Matthew 13:19 says: 'When anyone hears the message about the Kingdom and does not understand it, the evil one comes and snatches away what was sown in his heart.'

Children, or for that matter adults as well, need not only to hear the 'message of the Kingdom' but, as this verse suggests, to understand it as well. Obviously it is God the Holy Spirit who will bring understanding to people but the communicator also has a part to play in facilitating this process – good presentation and using language and concepts that are accessible to the listener are vital.

Teaching can very easily become boring and stereotyped and so it is important that the teacher is constantly asking God for creative ideas – he is, after all, the ultimate creator! Variety is definitely the spice of life so it is the responsibility of the teacher to use as many different forms of teaching as possible.

An old Chinese proverb says:

'I hear – and I forget,
I see – and I remember,
I do – and I understand.'

This gives a very valid commentary on the way that we learn. Any teaching that is done needs to include something of all these three aspects:

1. Hearing.
Verbal communication which needs to be clear and understandable.

2. Seeing.
This might mean using a prepared visual aid (see the Visual Aids section, page 111) or it could be an action or series of actions (mime).

3. Doing or application.
This will mean applying what has been learnt by doing something which would not have been possible before. It must be the aim of any teacher to get the students to a place where they have learnt something sufficiently well to be able to put it into practice. When talking in terms of spiritual teaching it needs to be such that people's lives are impacted and changed by what they hear.

In children's ministry it is probably fair to say that the most frequently used way of teaching spiritual truths is through a story (usually from the Bible).

STORYTELLING

All stories have an irresistible power. They trigger our creative imagination to enter the world of the story and become part of it. We see, feel and become part of the action. We stand beside the characters we like, willing them to come out on top; we recoil from the people we dislike, longing for them to meet their doom. And in the process we build our view of life. Sometimes the story confirms us in the attitudes we already hold; but sometimes it challenges us and opens us up to new possibilities.

Christian stories – and supremely, Bible stories – do all this and more. They show us God's way of looking at the world . . . And because God is present and active in his world, they help us find him there. (Lance Pierson in *Storytelling: A Practical Guide.*)

Storytelling is without doubt one of the most effective means of communication that exists. Stories appeal to young and old alike and can be used any time and anywhere. People will remember a story when they have forgotten everything else.

Jesus used this method of teaching throughout his earthly ministry, taking everyday situations and objects and building a story around them to communicate what was often a difficult spiritual truth. Those involved in children's ministry would do well to follow his example.

Stories can be used to:

a. create and hold interest

b. give information

c. introduce new ideas

d. present abstract truth in concrete life experiences

e. enable listeners to identify with real-life situations

f. relax and entertain listeners

Types of stories

1. Bible stories.

2. Real life stories, e.g. Corrie Ten Boom, Jackie Pullinger, personal testimonies.

3. Secular fictional stories which can be used to illustrate a point/truth/moral, e.g. the Mr Men, Popeye (without spinach he is weak, with it he is strong – similar to us with or without the Holy Spirit filling us).

4. Stories containing Christian principles or truths. These may be allegorical stories like *The Narnia* series by C. S. Lewis or just stories about ordinary everyday occurrences, e.g. *Treasures of the Snow* by Patricia St John.

Methods of storytelling

1. Tell the story using pre-prepared visual aids (see the section entitled Visual Aids, page 111).

2. Read (or tell) and dramatise (leaders or children can be the actors).

3. Pretend you are a character in the story and tell the story from that perspective.

4. All together drama (see example included in the Drama section, page 64).

5. Ilustrate the story as you tell it, or encourage the children to illustrate it as you tell it.

6. Use ladder lettering to reveal key words at various points in the story. (This has traditionally been used in conjunction with a sketch board presentation but is a useful technique in its own right.) It involves drawing the correct number of 'squares' for each word and then filling in the part of the letter which is usually missing.

7. Build up an acrostic using key words from the story, for example,

```
T A X C O L L E C T O R
      H O U S E
S Y C A M O R E T R E E
  M O N E Y
      G R E E D Y
    J E S U S
H A T E D
```

8. Use a puppet/s, e.g. a lamb, to tell the story of the lost sheep.

9. Use objects to represent key elements of a story, e.g. for the story of Zacchaeus you could have a small shirt (he was a small man), a purse or wallet (he was a tax collector), a twig (he climbed a tree), a cup of tea (Jesus went to his house for tea), money (he repaid those he had stolen from and gave 50 per cent of his money to the poor). If you can't get the actual objects then pictures of them work just as well.

10. 'Snip and tell'. Cut out a shape representing something from the story as you are actually telling it, revealing it at the appropriate time. The children could also be encouraged to do this. Construct your own or use already prepared ones as found in books such as *Snip and Tell Bible Stories* by Karyn Henley, or *Clip and Tell Bible Stories* by Lois Keffer, ISBN 1-55945-192-0 (published by Group Publishing, Box 485, Loveland, CO80539).

The above is by no means an exhaustive list but represents those which I have found to be the most useful in all kinds of different contexts.

Preparing to tell a story

1. Select the story, its length, its language and relevance to suit the age group.

2. Do some background reading so that you are able to set the story in context, e.g. how was it possible for the four friends in Mark 2 to make a hole in the roof in order to lower the paralysed man down to Jesus? What was the roof made from?

3. Decide on the storytelling method that you are going to use.

4. Read the story a number of times so that you are fully acquainted with all the details. In order to simplify something it is necessary to have a thorough, clear knowledge and understanding of the facts.

5. Make an outline of the story, numbering the incidents in order.

6. Think about and prepare visual aids where appropriate.

7. Practise your story so that you can tell it rather than read it.

Telling the story

1. Relax and be natural.

2. Enjoy the story yourself. The persuaded persuade – your own interest in the story and the way you tell it will determine how it will be received. Enthusiasm is contagious!

3. Vary the tone of your voice and don't be afraid to be dramatic. You are your best visual aid.

4. Maintain eye contact with your listeners, watch their reactions and modify your story if necessary.

5. Avoid long descriptions. Too many details can deaden the story while just the right amount can bring it to life.

6. Try to weave the spiritual application throughout the whole story as you tell it rather than leaving it to the end when the children's concentration and interest may wane.

7. Don't make it too long, remember concentration spans – one minute per year of age!

TEACHING BIBLICAL TRUTHS WITHOUT A STORY

Often there is not a single Bible story that will teach an actual truth or doctrine. It is at these times that there needs to be a great deal of reliance on the Lord to give the ideas that are necessary to teach these things in a creative and interesting way.

Objects

Sometimes it is possible to use either one object or a series of them to illustrate something, e.g.

Communion. This is about:

- Looking backwards and being thankful. Object = a cross.

- Looking inwards and asking for forgiveness for sin. Object = a mirror.

- Looking around and remembering that we are part of one body. Object = a family photograph.

- Looking forwards to when Jesus comes back and there is a wedding celebration. Object = a wedding invitation.

God wants to refresh and revive us by filling us with the Holy Spirit again and again.

Objects that could be used to introduce this include a pillow, an orange, a holiday brochure, a sponge, a packet of 'Refreshers', etc. – all are connected with refreshment of one sort or another.

When we are knocked, what we are full of will come out.

Fill up a cup so full of tea that when it is knocked it will easily spill. (Hudson Taylor used this to teach his new missionaries that it was very important to be full of God and not self, because when the hard times came, what they were full of would spill out.) For children a bottle of lemonade that is full and one that is only half full will perhaps be more relevant.

People

Sometimes it is possible to use individuals or groups of people to teach something specific. For example, when teaching about the work of the Holy Spirit, God's special helper, it can be a helpful introduction to look at some of the people that help us in our everyday lives (see section on Children and the Holy Spirit, page 23).

'Magic' tricks

These can be very useful but require a lot of practice to perfect technique, etc. Don't try them out with children until you are sure that you can do them and never give the secret of the trick away.

Movement/Mime

Teaching does not always have to be verbal in nature. Movement or mime can be an effective way of teaching. This can either be done by the leader or by the children. For example, instead of just teaching about the fruit of the Spirit, take each of the fruit in turn, love, joy, peace, patience, etc., and encourage the children to mime a stance or action to portray the opposite of each fruit. Then tell them to change to show the fruit itself, e.g. mime 'hate' – change into 'love'. To be able to do this, the children have to think about both the negatives and the positives and so teaching, and hopefully learning, occur as they go through the process.

Drama/Puppets

The presentation of drama and puppet sketches can introduce, teach or reinforce spiritual truths (see sections on Drama and Puppets, pages 64 and 91).

CONCLUSION

As can be seen from the above there are many different ways of teaching. Some are obviously more suited to the things being taught than others and it is necessary to make the combinations carefully. The responsibility of the teacher/ leader remains the same – to be as creative as possible, asking God for new ideas and working hard to present them to the highest possible standard.

Exercise 1

Look at Jesus the storyteller in the Gospels. What can be learnt by his approach?

Exercise 2

Take the story of Moses and the Burning Bush in Exodus 3. List as many different ways as you can of telling the story and illustrating it.

Exercise 3

Think of a truth that can be taught using the following objects:

Sponge

Blank piece of paper

Glove

Toothpaste tube

Apple

Counselling children

INTRODUCTION

In the last few years the amount of counselling available for adults, both within and outside the church, has greatly increased but there has not been anywhere near the increase where children are concerned. One only has to hear the statistics from Childline, detailing the number of children who phone in to talk about a whole range of problems to see that there are huge numbers of hurting children, who are desperately in need of receiving help and healing.

As Christians, we believe in a God who can bring healing and wholeness to adults and children alike as they reach out to him for help. However, while many churches have those who are experienced in counselling adults, few can offer any kind of effective counselling or help to a child who has some kind of 'substantial problem'. It is my belief that every church should have at least one person who is able to offer some help to needy children. It may be that a children's leader has the skills and anointing to do this, or it might be that a person who has counselling skills but not very much experience with children could work with a children's leader.

PRAYER MINISTRY/COUNSELLING

It is important at this stage to differentiate between what is often referred to as prayer ministry and counselling. Often when a person, child or adult, is touched by the Holy Spirit, problems lying just below the surface or that have been well and truly buried may come to the surface. Sometimes the problems are such that some extended prayer at the time, when the presence of God is strong, is enough for the person to receive considerable healing and help. There may need to be a small amount of follow-up counselling but the problem is largely dealt with by prayer ministry. On the other hand, some people's problems will warrant a session or more of counselling before they will receive the help which they need. It is important to ask God for wisdom as to the best course of action. If he deals with something quickly then that is great, but there is a need to be realistic and to work within the time frame that God dictates.

WHY COUNSEL CHILDREN?

It is possible to identify various stages of emotional development in a child. Failure to complete each stage can lead to an inability to develop properly. This means that many children who have experienced some trauma in their lives are not going to be able to reach full emotional development unless they receive appropriate help.

What tends to happen is that more and more layers of pain and hurt build up until, by the time the person reaches adulthood, prolonged counselling may be needed to begin to resolve their problems. If children receive counselling when situations arise and God's healing is experienced then they may well be spared the years of pain. However, this is not an area in which to get involved without the necessary skills and experience. More harm than good can be caused by those who perhaps try their hand at being a counsellor but who really don't know what they are doing. The message is clear, if in doubt, don't!

PROBLEMS THAT CHILDREN FACE

The problems that children face are as many and varied as are the reasons for them. They have the same needs and feelings as adults but often experience more confusion about things that happen in life. Below are just a few of the major problems that might be encountered in children.

- Physical, sexual and emotional abuse and neglect.

- Family break-up with all its associated problems including the children being convinced that it is their fault.

- Grief at the death of someone close to them (for some children even the death of a pet that perhaps they have grown up with can be very traumatic).

- Bullying – it is thought that just about every child will be bullied at some time during their school life.

- Moving home/area – children can face great loneliness, for example, because of a lack of friends.

- Fostering/adoption.

- Fears – most children have times when they are afraid of various things, but for some children a fear may grow to such an extent that they are 'paralysed' by it.

- Poor self-worth (this could be the result of such things as a lack of academic ability or dyslexia).

- Feelings of failure.

- Loneliness – an only child for instance, although greatly loved by its parents, can still feel very lonely.

- Illness of a family member, particularly if this is long-term.

SIGNS AND SYMPTOMS OF DISTRESS

Problems will present themselves in all kinds of different ways and it will often be necessary to ask God to reveal what the actual problem is. While some discipline problems are caused by poor programme content, many children, who are constantly disruptive, have significant underlying problems.

Some of the signs that *may* indicate that something is wrong include difficulty in concentrating, severe irritability, poor sleeping and eating habits, restlessness, disruptive behaviour, attention seeking, lack of spontaneity, nervous habits, frequent mood swings, excessive shyness, continually 'putting themselves down', attempting to take the blame when things go wrong, etc.

PRACTICAL CONSIDERATIONS

There is no doubt that, although many of the problems that children face are similar to those of adults, there are a number of different factors to be borne in mind when counselling children.

1. Children are very impressionable and it is vital that, in talking to them, they are not asked leading questions or have things 'planted' in their minds. This is important at all times and particularly so in the cases of child abuse.

2. Language/concepts used need to be carefully considered and age-appropriate.

3. Depending on a child's age and understanding the approach to counselling may be quite different. As Pauline Pearson says,

   Older children may be happy to sit and chat. Others will be more comfortable using paints, crayons, playdough, puppets, toy telephones, or whilst playing games, building with Duplo or Lego, looking at books or writing on a whiteboard. (*Counselling children* – Caring Summer, 1995.)

4. It may be appropriate to have a parent present, but there are also situations when this is not advisable, for instance in cases when the child's problem centres around their parents. At other times, problems may affect the whole family and there may need to be some work done with all the family members, individually and together.

   When the situation allows, it is good if counsellor and parents can work together to help the child.

5. It is important never to look for problems but rather to deal with things as and when they arise.

6. Once a child's problems have been exposed, it is vitally important that a counsellor works out with the child ways of coping. Many children whose parents separate and ultimately divorce are desperate for their mum and dad to get back together. While it would not be sensible in many cases to give the child the impression that this could happen or to pray along these

lines (although of course miracles do happen!), the child will need help to know how to cope with the situation as it is.

7. Whilst it is true in any dealings with children that an environment of trust, security, affirmation and encouragement needs to be created, it is even more so in the whole area of counselling.

8. Occasionally a child's problems will be the result of 'demonic' influences. Often children are much more aware of the enemy and his work than adults, so these times do not need to be ignored but rather handled sensitively. If prayer for deliverance is necessary, this should not be done in a loud or forceful way, which might unnecessarily frighten the child.

9. Every church needs to have a policy dealing with procedures to be adhered to if a child says that they have experienced abuse of some kind or even if it is just suspected. Various denominations have produced guidelines and PCCA Christian Child Care (PO Box 133, Swanley, Kent BR8 7UQ, telephone helpline 01322 660011) provide an advisory service and numerous extremely useful publications.

Counselling children is a huge subject and the above is not meant to be exhaustive but an attempt to highlight some of the most common questions. In all our attempts to help children, we must remember that, while what we do as Christians will obviously reflect our belief that God is the ultimate healer, there is much that we can learn from secular counselling methods.

Exercise 1

What would you do/say/pray, if a child came to you saying the following things?*

a. I'm always getting bullied at school.

b. Will you pray that I will know that God will heal me?

c. My mum says that I can't call my real dad, 'dad' any more, but I want to.

d. My parents don't care about me, my brother is the favourite.

e. My parents have split up and I really want them to get back together again. Will you pray for that?

* These are actual things that have been said to me, or members of my team.

Developing children's gifts and ministries

Church, WAKE UP! We NEED the children! They have unique talents and abilities that are necessary to the health of the whole Body – NOW, not someday when they grow up.

So writes Dian Layton in her book, *Soldiers with Little Feet.*

Children who are Christians are very much part of the church today, they have gifts and ministries that are vital to the healthy development of the Body. The responsibility of children's leaders is to help them to identify their particular gift or ministry and to release them into using it. Sometimes it is easy to see what a particular child's ministry might be but sometimes it is quite hidden and needs to be identified and brought out into the open.

The Bible identifies different kinds of gifts and ministries and there is a certain amount of overlap between them. The main passages to look at are 1 Corinthians 12:4-11, 27-30; Romans 12:4-8 and Ephesians 4:11-13.

1. *Natural talents and skills* that are in a sense God-given but are possessed by an individual whether they are a Christian or not (cf Exodus 31:1-7). A musical or artistic gift would fall into this category. For Christians such a gift is in the words of David Watson 'truly a gift of the Holy Spirit when it is used at God's inspiration, in God's power, for God's glory'. These natural gifts can obviously be used in all kinds of contexts but we need to encourage children to develop these and to use them for the benefit of others and to offer them as a resource for the Kingdom of God. We need to look for, or even create, the opportunity for children to use their talents, for example a child who has a musical gift could be used in the worship group/band in the main service or within the children's sessions. (Obviously a child will have to have reached a certain standard in order to do this but it is our responsibility first of all to discover what their abilities might be and then to encourage improvement so that they can use their talent in a church/Kingdom context).

2. *Spiritual gifts:* Phanerosis – manifestation of the Spirit (1 Corinthians 12:8-10), or charismata – gifts of grace (Romans 12:3-8). A gift that is sovereignly given to a believer by God. Children need to be taught what these gifts are, how to receive them, and given opportunity to practise using them.

3. *Ministries:* Diakoniai – ministries of the Spirit (1 Corinthians 12:28), or domata – equippers of the saints (Ephesians 4:8-14). A ministry is when a believer consistently and faithfully uses the same gift and this is recognised by others and referred to as a ministry. Some of the children that we have in our churches will be in this category and we have an enormous responsibility to help them to see this for themselves and then to make opportunities for them to exercise their ministries.

IDENTIFYING A CHILD'S GIFT OR MINISTRY

1. Ask God to show you.

2. Construct a questionnaire or use one like that included at the end of this section. These are best done on a one-to-one basis or with just a couple of children so that the leader or parent can help the child.

3. Make a list of indicators of possible ministries. (see Exercise 1).

4. Ensure that you know your children well.

5. Ask the children in your group to point out the things that each other are good at (this may give some clues, especially if the children know one another really well).

6. Talk to parents. Children's gifts will normally be much more obvious to them because of the amount of time that they spend with their children and the depth to which they know them.

HELPING CHILDREN TO FULFIL THEIR MINISTRIES

Opportunities to minister

It is no good recognising a child's gift or ministry if they are then not allowed to operate in it, as this will lead to frustration on the child's part. However it is risky! As Dian Layton says,

> I have wondered how many times we have missed the ministry of children because we were afraid of what they might do. It does take trust. It is a risk. They might say something inappropriate or do something wrong. SO?! If our nice, decent and in order services get shaken up from time to time – so what?! I think that encouraging the little members to move out in ministry would have results that far surpass the odd little embarrassment they might cause!

Developing children's gifts

It is important to remember that as children get older, their ministries may well change and develop, and allowances will need to be made for this. Allow children the freedom for such development.

Build in review/evaluation times – how well is the child doing? How well are you doing at giving opportunities to minister?

Training also needs to be provided for them where appropriate, e.g. a training course in evangelism for our young evangelists!

Spirituality versus gifting

Careful attention needs to be paid, not just to how well children are doing at using their gifts, but also how they are doing spiritually. In Brownsville, Pensacola, the children's church is run by the children. A training manual has been produced that outlines what is expected of children who are going to minister, e.g. they have to have a good relationship with the Lord, be committed to prayer, Bible reading and worship as well as go to practices and be good timekeepers, etc. Don't be afraid to ask a child to stop ministering if they are struggling spiritually but be careful how you approach this. Be positive by encouraging the child to sort out their relationship with God rather than making them feel bad about not ministering. Tell them that most people need to take a break at some point and concentrate on themselves, and let them know that they can minister again when things change.

Finally we need to ensure that the children have a right view of the gifts and ministries that they have. They must constantly realise that they are God-given and that they must guard against pride and elitism as Alan Price says in his book *Children in Renewal* (Kevin Mayhew, 2000):

> God gives these things out of love for us and his Church and because he wants us to be useful to him in bringing about his purposes in the world. We are 'saved to serve', following the example of Jesus.

Vann Lane, the children's pastor at Brownsville, Pensacola, in Florida, says the following in his book, *Children of Revival*,

> I am looking forward with great anticipation toward the future. What benefits we will reap from providing the children with opportunities to discover and nurture their God-given talents and abilities! In a few years we will not have to go outside the church to find spiritual, mature, trained and experienced people in any area of ministry. A group of committed, solid young ministers will be standing before us saying, 'Here am I. Send me.'

Ephesians 4:16 says, 'So when each separate part works as it should, the whole body grows and builds itself up through love', – that surely means children as well as adults!

Exercise 1

Draw lines between the gifts/ministries and the possible indicators of these.

PROPHECY	Debbie is always bringing different friends to church.
SERVING	Susan would always give her last 'Rolo' away.
TEACHING	Simon always makes constructive contributions when his group is planning a special event.
ENCOURAGING	Jane often receives and shares 'pictures' from God.
GIVING	Philip is always asking questions about the Bible.
LEADERSHIP	Christopher always enjoys it when his parents invite people for Sunday lunch.
SHOWING MERCY/SYMPATHY	Sally always wants to give out the felt tips.
EVANGELISM	James is quick to help those who are struggling.
HOSPITALITY	John likes to 'take over' whenever possible.
ADMINISTRATION	Jenny likes to comfort people if they are upset.

Now make your own list of indicators.

PROPHECY

SERVING

TEACHING

ENCOURAGING

GIVING

LEADERSHIP

SHOWING MERCY/SYMPATHY

EVANGELISM

HOSPITALITY

ADMINISTRATION

Exercise 2

Taking the list of gifts/ministries below, think of ways in which you could give opportunity for them to be used.

PROPHECY

SERVING

TEACHING

ENCOURAGING

GIVING

LEADERSHIP

SHOWING MERCY/SYMPATHY

EVANGELISM

HOSPITALITY

ADMINISTRATION

Discover your ministry

Read the statements in each section and then circle a number for each one.

0 = least like you; 5 = most like you. Be honest!

1. Leader	0 1 2 3 4 5
2. Teacher	0 1 2 3 4 5
3. Intercessor	0 1 2 3 4 5
4. Evangelist	0 1 2 3 4 5
5. Prophet	0 1 2 3 4 5
6. Pastor/Counsellor/Encourager	0 1 2 3 4 5
7. Showing mercy	0 1 2 3 4 5
8. Hospitality	0 1 2 3 4 5

1. LEADER

You are often chosen to be the leader.
People copy what you do.
You like to be in charge and sometimes you can be bossy.

2. TEACHER

You like to explain things and make sure that others understand them.
You like finding out things, e.g. what the Bible means.
Other people often ask you questions.

3. INTERCESSOR

You like praying/you pray a lot on your own, as well as with other people.
Sometimes you feel sad, like God does, about things that are happening in the world.
You really believe that God can change things when you pray.

4. EVANGELIST

You love to tell people about Jesus.
You feel concerned that people may not go to heaven.
Even though you may sometimes feel scared, you still tell people about Jesus.
All your friends know that you love Jesus and go to church.

5. PROPHET

You often receive pictures/visions/dreams/words from God.
You often think you know what God is saying or feeling.
You're not afraid to share things that God tells you, even though some people might not like it or understand.

6. PASTOR/COUNSELLOR/ENCOURAGER

People talk to you about their problems.
You like to cheer people up and encourage them.
You are good at listening to people and try to help them whenever you can.
You like to see people trusting God more.

7. SHOWING MERCY

You feel sad when you see poor/homeless people.
You feel that you want to do something to help them.
Sometimes when you see starving people/people who are suffering on the TV, you keep thinking about them.
You like to give money to people in need.

8. HOSPITALITY

You like it when people come to your house to visit or to stay.
You like to make cookies/cakes for others.
When people come to your house, you like to make sure that they have a really good time.
You don't mind giving up your room and letting others share your things.

DIY – writing your own material

Why not have a go at writing your own teaching material? Perhaps try it for two or three months initially – you may be surprised at the creative ideas that emerge! There are definite advantages in 'tailor-made' material although as with anything there are also a few disadvantages.

Advantages

1. The specific needs of your group can be more easily met.

2. Saves money!

3. Takes into consideration the gifts and abilities of leaders.

4. Encourages creativity in leaders and stimulates enthusiasm.

5. More flexibility is possible.

6. Children can have the same 'diet' of teaching as the adults in a church when appropriate.

7. A basic plan can be adapted for all ages of children if desired.

8. Less possibility of becoming stale, predictable, boring and irrelevant

Disadvantages

1. All visual aids and 'take-home' papers need to be home-produced.

2. The on-going need for creativity and new ideas.

3. Initially it can take more time and effort.

4. Difficulties in working out an overall plan.

WHAT ABOUT AN OVERALL PLAN?

It is important that there is a well-balanced overall plan of teaching content. This needs to be long term and cater for different ages, in order to avoid repetition as children change groups. Many people would prefer to write their own material, but the thought of planning such an overall scheme can be a daunting task and so resorting to using published material, where this is already produced, becomes a very attractive option.

However, constructing an overall plan may not be as complex as it at first appears.

The following points need to be considered:

1. Repetition.
Generally speaking, repetition needs to be kept to a minimum. Therefore it is not always advisable for some groups within a Sunday School to follow published schemes while others are using 'home produced' material. If this is the case, then close liaison is necessary between the leaders of different age groups.

Some subjects do need to be repeated, e.g. the need for salvation, whereas a favourite story such as Zacchaeus can become rather boring if this is the tenth time that you have heard it!

To limit repetition of content, the best course of action is for each group to follow the same basic plan, adapting it to suit various age groups, although this will not always be appropriate.

2. Content.
To be able to plan long-term, i.e. three or four years in advance is the ideal, although there will always be a need for flexibility and a willingness to change.

However, don't worry if you can't plan so far in advance. Start by asking the Lord to show you any specific teaching series that the children might need at that particular time. If nothing becomes clear, then choose your first theme, Bible book or character, taking into account the needs of the children. In planning subsequent series continually refer back in order to keep a good balance. The overall plan will then gradually unfold.

N.B. It is important to keep accurate and dated records of teaching content and programmes, for the benefit of future leaders.

The responsibility for creating or developing the overall plan is probably best left to a few suitably gifted people. These could be representatives from each age grouping but need not necessarily be so.

However, even if you do not feel you want to write your own material long-term you may feel that you need to ring the changes and depart from the ready-made curriculum for a short period. It may be that you see a specific area which needs addressing and therefore it is good to know how to build your own programme.

PLANNING A SERIES

1. Length of series will vary but it is advisable not to make them too long, especially with younger children. (Between three and six sessions would be average.)

2. Choose the subject material for a series and then 'brainstorm' it. It may be:

   a. *A theme or topic*, e.g. forgiveness, obedience, fruit of the Spirit, a Psalm. In these cases there is an overall teaching point but often there can be more than one aspect to it – e.g. forgiveness could have two major points – God forgives us/We need to forgive others. The number of different aspects will determine the length of the series. The next step is to select relevant Bible stories, memory verses, songs, activities, etc.

   b. *A Bible character*, e.g. Moses, Jonah, Peter, etc. In these cases the story content is already obvious but the story subject matter will have to be divided into relevant sections. Then a teaching point needs to be decided upon for each session and finally suitable memory verses, songs, puppets, dramas, crafts, etc., selected.

   c. *A Bible book* (or part of one), e.g. Psalms, Proverbs, James, etc. It may be that you would want to give the children an overview of a particular book or a few chapters of a book. Again, story content and teaching points will need to be decided upon.

Below is an example of planning a series about the life of Moses for 3-11 year olds.

1. A series of about four to six weeks was thought to be right. Six weeks were selected for 7-11s and four weeks for for 3-6s

2. The story of Moses up to the crossing of the Red Sea was read. (Exodus, chapters 1-14.)

3. Appropriate stories and relevant incidents were selected.

4. A teaching point for each session was decided.

5. A six-week series was planned, of which perhaps only four would be selected for the 3-6s.

Week 1

Bible base	Exodus 2:1-10
Story	Baby in a Basket
Teaching point	
(7-11s)	God has plans for us even when we are very young
(3-7s)	God wants to keep us safe
Memory verse	
(7-11s)	Jeremiah 29:11b – 'I have good plans for you. I don't plan to hurt you. I plan to give you hope and a good future.'
(3-7s)	1 Peter 5:7 – '. . . He cares for you.'

Week 2

Bible base	Exodus 2:11-15
Story	Run for your life! (Moses and the Egyptian)
Teaching point	
(7-11s)	God forgives our mistakes
(3-7s)	Doing wrong and being sorry
Memory verse	
(7-11s)	1 John 1:9 – 'But if we confess our sins to God he will keep his promise and do what is right.'
(3-6s)	Acts 3:19b – 'Come back to God and he will forgive your sins.'

Week 3

Bible base	Exodus 3:1-14
Story	Help! I can't do it! (Moses and the burning bush)
Teaching point	
(3-11s)	God is our helper
Memory verse	
(3-11s)	Psalm 118:7a – 'The Lord is with me. He is my helper.'

Week 4

Bible base	Exodus 5-10
Story	Never give up! (The ten plagues)
Teaching point	
(3-11s)	Perseverance

Memory verse
(7-11s) — Acts 18:9b – 'Do not be afraid. Keep on speaking. Do not be silent.'

(3-6s) — Matthew 7:7a – 'Continue to ask and God will give to you . . .'

Week 5
Bible base — Exodus 11-12
Story — Get ready (The Passover)
Teaching point
(3-11s) — Following God's instructions
Memory verse
(3-6s) — Matthew 4:19 – 'Jesus said, "Follow me"'
(7-11s) — Matthew 7:24 – 'Everyone who hears these things I say and obeys them is like a wise man.'

Week 6
Bible base — Exodus 13:17-14:31
Story — The great escape (Crossing the Red Sea)
Teaching Point
(3-11s) — Nothing is too hard for God
Memory verse
(7-11s) — Jeremiah 32:27 – 'I am the Lord, the God of all mankind. Is anything too hard for me?'
(3-6s) — Luke 1:37 – 'God can do everything!'

N.B. Scripture verses were included in each session but the children were not expected to learn them all!

Having worked out this basic plan, the next step was to add songs for praise and worship, any art and craft activity, games, quizzes, drama, puppets, group times for discussion/prayer that might be appropriate. Then six programmes were drawn up.

Example – Week 1 for 3-6 year olds. Teaching Point: God looks after us

TIME (approx)	INGREDIENTS	3-6s
11:00	Praise	Two suitable praise songs were chosen.
11:05	Teaching	The story of 'Moses in the Bullrushes' was told using OHP pictures as a visual aid.
11:15	Memory verse 1 Peter 5:7 'He cares for you.'	5 pictures of 'things we need' (e.g. food, drink, clothing, mum and dad, sun), were mounted on pieces of card. On the back of each was written one word of the Scripture verse, not forgetting the reference. 5 children were chosen to hold up the pictures while they were discussed, and then the cards were turned round to show the Scripture verse. The verse was read and then learned by asking at random one of the children to turn their card over and asking the children if they could still say the verse. The process was repeated until all the pictures were showing again.
11:25	Interactive drama	'Noah' (Taken from *Play On Words*)
11:35	Worship	Two songs were sung. 'No, No, No, I Will Never, Never Leave You' and 'Jesus Says, "Keep Close"' (Both taken from *Powerpack Praise*)
	Response	Children closed their eyes and hugged themselves and 'imagined' Jesus holding them close. Leader prayed for the children.
11:42	Craft	Children made their own collage pictures, using pre-prepared cut out pictures of 'things we need'. The pictures were stuck onto large sheets of sugar paper on which was already written 'Thank You God for . . .'
11:50	Prayer	The children used their collage pictures to thank God for caring for them. They also prayed for poor and sad children.
11:55	Praise	Two more songs of praise and thanksgiving were sung.

Exercise 1

Write out a programme for 7-11 year olds for Week 1 of the above series with the teaching point, 'God has plans for us'.

TIME	INGREDIENTS	7-11s

Exercise 2

Now write your own basic plan for a teaching series. Choose one of the following themes, topics or characters. Start by 'brainstorming' all the possibilities.

RUTH   GOD THE HOLY SPIRIT   PSALM 139   FAITH   PAUL

Planning a series

WHAT DOES GOD WANT TO SAY
TO THE CHILDREN?

WHAT DO THE CHILDREN NEED TO
KNOW OR EXPERIENCE?

CHOOSE THE SUBJECT MATERIAL
– a theme or topic, character or Bible book

DECIDE ON THE LENGTH OF THE SERIES

CHOOSE A TEACHING POINT FOR EACH SESSION

SELECT THE RELEVANT SCRIPTURES

DECIDE ON BIBLE VERSES, SONGS, ACTIVITIES, PUPPETS & DRAMA

PLAN A WEEKLY PROGRAMME

Discipline

Discipline – the very word can trigger clammy palms and elevated heart rates in both teachers and kids. But it doesn't need to be that way. No teacher wants to be a drill sergeant. No child wants to be in trouble all the time.

What do teachers want? Classrooms full of kids who are excited to be in church, busily engaged in meaningful learning and motivated to stay on task. What do kids want? Exactly the same thing. (*The Discipline Guide For Children's Ministry*)

Too many volunteer leaders 'give up' because of discipline problems while many potential leaders never even volunteer because of fears of not being able to control the children that they will be asked to lead. Our thinking needs to change to see that discipline, which comes from the root word 'disciple', is just that – 'discipling', and is a positive process of training rather than a negative one of punishment. Good 'discipline is an ongoing process in which teacher control gradually gives way to Christian self-control, or should we say, God control' (*The Discipline Guide for Children's Ministry*). Children need help to see that discipline is actually positive even though they don't like it (Hebrews 12:11).

CHILDREN BY NATURE ARE SINFUL

Genesis 8:21: '. . . every inclination of his heart is evil from childhood.'

Proverbs 29:15: 'The rod of correction imparts wisdom but a child left to himself disgraces his mother.'

God is a God of order and discipline and the children need to know this both by what we say and what we do. 1 Corinthians 14:33: 'For God is not a God of disorder but of peace.'

GOD'S INSTRUCTIONS

Proverbs 13:24: 'He who spares the rod hates his son, but he who loves him is careful to discipline him.'

Proverbs 23:13-14: 'Do not withhold discipline from a child; if you punish him with the rod he will not die. Punish him with the rod and save his soul from death.'

Proverbs 22:15: 'Folly is bound up in the heart of a child, but the rod of discipline will drive it far from him.'

WHY IS IT IMPORTANT?

Children like it and need it!

It shows a loving, caring attitude and helps the child to feel secure.

It is honouring to the Lord.

WHAT SHOULD WE EXPECT?

Good but reasonable standards. Set limits that are attainable.

OUR PART

1. Plan a good, balanced programme. Interest, enjoyment and involvement mean that the children don't want to misbehave. Ensure that concentration spans are considered when planning a programme.

2. Be well prepared.

3. Be consistent. (Decide on the rules and keep to them at every session and with every child.)

4. Take control of the situation. Be firm but loving.

5. Involve the children as much as possible.

6. Be aware of potential danger points, e.g. before and after sessions, prayer times, quizzes, during action songs, between programme items.

7. Never threaten something that you cannot carry out.

8. Give clear understandable instructions.

9. Try to involve the ringleader as a helper.

10. Play on their good nature.

11. Be friendly and show an interest in them.

12. Laugh with the children but not at them.

13. Pray and encourage others to do the same.

14. Look at the reasons why a child is causing problems and address the cause rather than the symptoms. Refer to parents. The ultimate step of exclusion may be necessary as a last resort if the rest of the group are suffering.

DO NOT

a. Smack them! Be very careful about any form of physical contact.

b. Show irritation, anger, fear or embarrassment.

c. Get involved in a shouting contest.

d. Label children.

e. Shame and blame and make a child feel devalued.

f. Give directions in the form of a question. In other words don't ask a child if they would like to sit down and listen because they might well say no!

REMEMBER

Good discipline is much harder to create than to maintain.

Where God is at work, Satan will want to disrupt. Resist him and he will flee (James 4:7).

PRACTICAL TECHNIQUES

Every group of children and every situation is, of course, very different. Often with a difficult group it is necessary to try a variety of methods. Here are some suggestions:

1. *Teams* – divide the children into teams (the number of teams will obviously vary according to the size of the group). Give points for responding to instructions and deduct points for wrong behaviour. Be creative and score in different ways.

2. *Balloon Pop* – blow up three balloons for each team and pop one every time children misbehave. (Obviously with only three balloons you can only pop them when something of a more serious nature occurs).

3. *Coloured card system* – adopt a system like that used in football when a yellow card is given as a warning and a red one when the behaviour is such that it warrants being sent off. (Three yellow cards would equal a red card, at which point the child would be excluded for a week and the parents would need to be informed.)

4. *Whistle/squeaker* – use a whistle/squeaker to act as a sign that the children should be quiet or do something else that is pre-arranged.

5. *Role reversal* – let children prepare and present part of the programme. You might find children that are potential leaders and they will realise how difficult it is when children constantly misbehave.

6. *Exercise time* – this is particularly useful if you are working within a confined space. Give the children instructions such as stand up, stand on one leg, put one hand in the air, etc. This just provides a very short distraction and gives the children time to use up a little excess energy. Obviously if you have more space the exercises can be even more energetic.

7. *Contracts* – draw up a contract with a child whereby they agree to try harder in certain areas of behaviour, e.g.

_____ (Child's name)   Date _____

I will try to do better at

1. _____

2. _____

3. _____

Signed _____ leader
        _____ child
        _____ parent

8. People placement
   a. Tell 'chatty' friends that sitting together is a privilege that they will have to cease to enjoy if they talk when they are not supposed to.

   b. Put quiet children where they will receive lots of eye contact, which seems to act as non-verbal permission to talk, and noisy children at the sides where they will not get so much direct eye contact.

9. Give children the opportunity to talk about and decide what the rules should be.

Exercise 1
Define discipline

Exercise 2
What is the purpose of discipline?

Exercise 3
What should be the goal of discipline in the church?

Exercise 4
What things cause children to misbehave?

Drama

The emphasis in many churches is often on children practising and 'performing' a piece of drama for the monthly family service, Christmas, Easter, etc. While there can be value in this, especially if done well, drama has a much wider usage than this. When leaders 'take to the stage' drama can become a powerful teaching tool. If you don't have any leaders gifted in this area invite others who are not your regular children's workers to join you and use their skills.

DRAMA IS VALUABLE

a. It is visual . . . we see and we remember.

b. It suits all ages and abilities.

c. It can be very relevant using ordinary everyday experiences.

d. It can involve the children either directly or by identification.

DRAMA CAN BE USED . . .

a. To teach or explain.

b. To initiate, provoke or stimulate.

c. To reinforce.

d. To entertain.

Tips

1. Keep scripts simple, short and relevant.

2. Use easily understood language.

3. Don't explain everything! The meaning of the sketch does not have to be explained within the sketch, but can be taken up in another way, at another time.

4. Be seen and heard. When performing you must be heard and seen clearly. Gestures, faces, movements, etc., need to be exaggerated.

5. Be well prepared.

6. Remember that drama involves the whole person – it's not just about learning lines!

DRAMA AS AN ACTIVITY FOR CHILDREN

Many children enjoy drama but will never make great actors! However, they can be part of a drama activity and have great fun just 'having a go'.

1. Drama exercises.
These are just general exercises to get the children to think about movements, sounds, working together, etc. Here is an example taken from *100+ Ideas for Drama*, by Anna Scher and Charles Verrall which will make the children think out their reactions and movements.

Each child has a chair. Ask the children to stand up and then tell them something about their chair, e.g. it's smelly! They then have to act sitting on their chair knowing this fact. Other things that could be suggested about the chair are that it is: sticky, not safe, hot, covered in invisible itching powder, next to someone they don't like, uncomfortable, forbidden to sit on!

2. Dramatised stories.
Read (from a version suitable for children) or tell the story. Choose stories which are suitable for the number of children in your group. For example, in the story of the 'Stilling of the Storm' some children can take the parts of the main characters and the remainder can be involved by sitting in the shape of a boat or making sound effects, etc. Consequently this is suitable for quite a large group. Of course, small group time gives opportunity for this type of drama activity too.

3. Interactive Bible stories.
Rewrite a Bible story assigning actions to various words. Then read the story and everyone does the actions. (See example at end of this section.)

General tips when working with children

1. Try to involve the majority of the children most of the time.

2. Encourage children to be involved but don't put pressure on them.

3. Give clear instructions.

4. Introduce a fun element whenever possible.

5. Be well prepared.

    a. Use simple props or just pretend.

    b. Think about the available space and how you will use it.

    c. Plan beforehand which children could play which part.

6. Don't expect a polished end result – the enjoyment is in the doing.

Points to remember when performing a drama

- The way you move, stand, sit.
- Think about stature, facial expression, gesture and voice.
- Think about how you relate to objects, e.g. when picking up a suitcase which is supposed to be full, make it look as though it is!
- Think about how you relate to other actors.
- Exaggerate but be believable – thinking yourself into the role.
- Allow some time – reactions are not always immediate. (Children will often need to do something twice.)
- Take your time – don't rush your lines or speak too fast. Relax!

Exercise 1

You are having a telephone conversation. Using only the words 'Yes', 'No' and 'Oh' express the following:

1. Hearing gossip.
2. Hearing bad news.
3. Hearing good news.
4. You're being asked to do something you don't want to do!
5. You are being given directions.
6. You are being accused unfairly.

Exercise 2

Walk or move in such a way to show that you are:

Angry, happy, sad, waiting for someone who is late, locked in, in love, worried, in a panic!

Exercise 3

Take the story of Zacchaeus and write your own interactive Bible story. Think of the age group for which you are writing it – if for young children make the actions literal but if for older children incorporate some 'play on words'.

Exercise 4

Look up the parable of 'The Sower' in Matthew 13:1-9. Work out a mime that could accompany the story as it is read straight from the Bible.

All together drama
Adam and Eve

Teaching points
- temptation
- disobedience

Adam *** *(Boys march left, right, on the spot)* and Eve *** *(Girls march left, right, on the spot)* lived a long, lo . . . ng *** *(Say 'long' slowly and stretch out arms)* time *** *(Look at watch)* ago, in a beautiful garden *** *(Kiss fingers, Italian chef style!)*. Everything was really good *** *(Thumbs up!)* and God *** *(Point upwards)* walked *** *(Walk on the spot)* in the garden *** and talked *** *(Talking action with hand)* with Adam *** and Eve *** every day.

They were very happy *** *(Hilarious silent laughter)* in the garden ***, but God *** had told them *** *(Wag finger in telling-off fashion)* that there was one thing *** *(Show one finger)* they must not do *** *(Shake head)* – eat the fruit *** *(Eat fruit noisily, rub tummy)* of the tree *** *(Make an unusual tree shape!)* in the middle of the garden ***. If they did then they would die *** *(Die dramatically with suitable sound effects)*.

One day, a serpent *** *(Wiggle arm, say, 'Ssssss'!)* came and told Eve *** it was OK *** *(Thumbs up)* to eat the fruit ***, and that they would not die ***. So *** *(Sew)* she picked the fruit *** *(Pick fruit from tree)* and ate it ***. Then she gave some *** *(Give to someone)* to Adam *** who ate it *** as well.

Soon God *** came into the garden ***. He said, 'Where are you *** *(Look around, hand across eyes)*, Adam ***? Where are you ***, Eve ***?' Adam *** and Eve *** were hiding *** *(Turn away, arms over head)*. They felt ashamed *** *(Cover face with hands)* and guilty *** *(Fearful, biting nails)*. They knew they had done wrong and they didn't want to see *** *(Look through binoculars)* God ***.

God *** knew *** *(Point to side of head)* what they had done and was very sad *** *(Cry dramatically)*. Everything that was so good *** was now so bad *** *(Thumbs down)*. He would have to put Adam *** and Eve *** out of the garden now *** *(Point to one side)* and no more would they be close friends *** *(Join own hands together in front of you)*. What was he going to do now *** *(Shrug shoulders)*?

Family services

Family services, or all-age services as they have become commonly known, are those in which children and adults remain together for the whole of the service time. Many churches may not have regular 'family services' but the whole body of the church, including children, meet together for part of a service. The principles outlined in these notes need to be applied in both these situations.

MISCONCEPTIONS ABOUT FAMILY SERVICES

1. Just being together as families does not constitute a family service.

2. They are not just children's services to which adults are allowed or forced to attend.

3. They are not adult services with a children's section.

4. They are not just the chance to see the latest piece of drama that the children have practised in Sunday School.

5. They are not the solution to the problem of not having enough leaders for the Sunday School. As Jackie Cray says:

   The family service solved a problem for many church leaders who were finding it difficult to recruit regular committed leaders for their children's work . . . Many churches solved the problem by keeping the children in with them. But it wasn't really all-age anything! It was merely a conventional service with something slotted in for the children without necessarily altering any of the rest of the service structure.

A true family service should be a time when everybody, whatever their age, can enter into worship and prayer, where they can receive teaching from the word of God, be involved in ministering to one another (yes that does mean children to adults as well as vice versa!) as well as having fun together. More importantly there needs to be a genuine expectation that God is wanting to work powerfully as opposed to an emphasis on trying 'to keep everybody happy'.

To achieve the above is not an easy task. To start with the mere suggestion of a family service stirs up all kinds of reactions. The children think it will be boring and would rather be in their own groups, the adults think it will be childish and superficial, older people may think it will be too active and noisy, teenagers feel that there is going to be nothing in it for them and the pastor finds the choice of content a real headache! In addition:

> *For many single people, the word 'family', especially in a church context, has an amazing ability to press the paranoia button . . . For a surprisingly high proportion of Christians, I'd guess that the word 'family' gives a message that's as unmistakable as it is unintentional: 'You are not included.'* (Jackie Cray)

SO WHY DO WE BOTHER?

1. We have been called together to be the family of God. God commands blessing when we dwell together in unity (Psalm 133).

2. It is good for children to feel included in the full life of the church. To be in a place where they are made to feel loved, secure and significant.

3. Adults can be positive role models for children in worship, etc.

4. Child-like faith can be a great stimulus to adults.

5. So that at particular times the church family can together hear and respond to what God is saying and doing.

IMPORTANT FACTORS FOR A SUCCESSFUL FAMILY SERVICE

1. With different age groups having such diverse characteristics and needs, it is impossible for every element of a family service to be applicable to everybody. To recognise this from the outset is vital.

2. The choice of theme is crucial. The subject needs to be applicable and challenging to children through to the older members of the church. It must be clearly presented in a variety of ways throughout the whole service. Everybody should go away knowing exactly what God has said.

3. A gifted leader is vital. Someone with an understanding of both children and adults, who has the ability to involve everybody, and a heart to see God work in the whole church family.

4. A team of committed people who have skills in particular areas, e.g. drama, puppets, music, etc.

5. Children respond to activity, action and variety and this must be borne in mind as well as the fact that their concentration spans are short.

6. Children need more help than adults to know at what point they can participate, e.g. in prayer, sharing anything that they may receive from God, etc.

7. A mixture of songs needs to be used with explanation for the children where necessary and encouragement to participate for the adults.

8. Be sensitive to teenagers. There is a need to think of ways to help them feel a part of what is going on.

9. Above all else there must be 'give and take' on the part of both the adults and the children.

Regular family services are the ideal but it will be necessary to work within your resources. As in any family, adults and children need times apart as well as together. However, in my opinion it is vital that there are times in a church context when we come together, but this time MUST be quality time, time that the whole family enjoys and benefits from. We need to ask God for inspiration and enabling to make our family services an exciting time, when God is not only present but clearly at work.

Exercise 1

Make a list of activities suitable for 'family services'. Some will be more suitable for children and some for adults but work out how you can make them work for all the ages. A talk that is aimed at adults, which uses some form of visual aid or contains examples that are applicable to children and youth is a good example.

Exercise 2

Make a list of currently used songs which are accessible to both children and adults (don't forget the teenagers).

Family service example: Too busy for God

AN EXAMPLE OF A FAMILY SERVICE

Welcome/Introduction

Game

Heavy laden?

Two volunteers were asked for (adults), and each was loaded up with various objects representing all the possible activities in which we can be involved. The object of the game is to see who can hold the most without dropping a single item. You will need two lots of objects, one set for each contestant. Find objects to represent things like the need to go to work, to sleep, spend time with family, wash, iron, clean, cook, shop, keep fit, relax, decorate, do the gardening, attend meetings, watch TV, listen to Sunday's Service, do some DIY. Have a diary asking the question 'When am I free?' and finally, when it's obviously impossible to hold anything else, present them with a Bible! The point is clear!

Children could be used and the objects chosen appropriately

Set the theme/Prayer

Praise

Praise songs were chosen appropriate for both children and adults. No more than 10 minutes.

Puppets

Too busy for people

One puppet is planning a surprise birthday party for a friend. He phones round imaginary puppets who offer various excuses as to why they are unable to come – one will miss his favourite TV programme, one wants to play football and one has a new computer game and can't leave it!

Offering

A suitable worship song was sung during this time.

Drama

Too busy to pray

Drama depicts a day in the life of a young teenager. Begins in bed, then alarm goes, dozes off to sleep again, wakes with a start, picks up his Bible and puts it down again unread, has a quick wash, dresses and is off to do a paper round. Returns home, has breakfast, gathers books, cleans teeth and off to school. Day passes quickly at school, bell goes and it's hometime at last! Arrives home, sits watching TV, goes out to play football, comes in for tea, time for homework and then to bed. Gets into bed and then remembers prayers. Gets out of bed and kneels down and says, 'Our Father . . .' at which point a 'voice' answers him as if it were God speaking directly to him. Points out God's desire to talk to him and lovingly points out all the opportunities he had missed to make time for God. Boy decides to do better next day.

Scripture verse game

Luke 10:27

The Scripture verse was written out on card (x2), cut into about 10-12 jigsaw pieces and hidden under the seats/pews before the service. The congregation was divided into two halves and two adults/teenagers chosen from each team to make the puzzle. Then at the appropriate signal, each team had to find the pieces and bring them to the front. (This could be a job for everyone or just for the children.) The first team to complete the puzzle (sticking the pieces down onto a board with blu-tac) was the winner!

Worship

Love the Lord your God (based on the Scripture verse)*

Jesus reign in me (+ one more song well known to adults)*

*Both these songs may be found on the Powerpack cassette *Worship the King* which has an accompanying music book – available from The Powerpack Trust or Christian bookshops.

Talk/Story

Mary and Martha
OHP pictures of the story to illustrate the talk.
(Duration approx. 10 minutes)

Song

Keep Close (presentation song about the need to stay close to Jesus)*

Response

Time for individual response to the word/to receive ministry if appropriate.

Final song

A suitable song of dedication/resolve.

* The song 'Keep Close' is on the cassette *On the Track with Powerpack* and is included in the *Powerpack Praise* bumper music book (available from The Powerpack Trust).

Go then . . .
Evangelism with children

Evangelism is bringing people face to face with Jesus Christ who died for them. It is showing people the way to God the Father, through preaching about Jesus, by the power of the Holy Spirit. Put in simple terms it is finding children and telling them about Jesus.

Jesus came to 'seek and save the lost' and he calls his people to be those who are following in his footsteps. He was always sensitive to people, meeting them where they were and speaking in terms that they could understand. In order to reach adults and children alike it is vital that we learn from the approach of Jesus. Love dominated and directed everything he did and any evangelism of children must be characterised by the same kind of love.

EVANGELISM AMONGST CHILDREN IS VALID AND VITAL

In the 41 Billy Graham meetings during 'Mission England' in 1984 there was a high percentage of 'enquirers' at all meetings, and of these 9 per cent were aged 10 or under (44 per cent boys), while 18 per cent were aged 11-13 years (41 per cent boys). 74 per cent of those aged 10 or under and 68 per cent of those aged 11-13 said that they wished to accept Jesus Christ as personal Saviour, as against just under 47 per cent of adults. (Children In The Way)

Research has shown that in the USA 85 per cent of people become Christians between the ages of 4 and 14. It is not known whether this is the case in other parts of the world but it seems likely.

Dr Dan Brewster, in a paper that he wrote in 1996 entitled 'The "4-14" Window Child Ministries

and Mission Strategy', says that,

> *cutting edge mission groups today are making some of the most significant advances in the history of Christianity by looking at the '10-40' Window . . . There is another 'window within a window, however, which may be just as significant . . . the '4-14' window.*

Despite the fact that this group may be one of the most fruitful mission fields, it is often largely neglected, particularly when planning future church strategy. In 1966 Wolfe Hansen wrote that,

> *the time has come to make the younger generation our prime objective in evangelism. To neglect it would be a strategic blunder. (Evangelical Missions Quarterly, Summer 1966).*

Yet the situation is still largely the same.

The tide is beginning to turn and more churches are taking this mission field seriously. It is important, however, that churches start to strategically plan how they are going to reach the children in their neighbourhoods – it won't just happen! A 'holiday club' once a year is not sufficient!

CONTEXTS FOR EVANGELISM

1. Sunday activities.
This is a difficult time since non-Christians often engage in other activities on a Sunday and also because in split families children may go to the other parent at weekends. Also, children often remain in the adult service for a short period of time before going out to their children's groups. This can be difficult for children from non-church families to cope with and also presents problems of supervision.

2. Midweek activities.
These could take a number of forms:

a. Uniformed organisations (often single sex and a mixture of activities.

b. Activity based club with a 'Christian slot'.

c. Activity based club with no overt Christian content. (Often these clubs have an emphasis on relationship building with the children, with the hope that they will, at some point, attend some more overtly Christian event in the church.)

d. Christian club with a magazine style programme (i.e. a fast-moving programme consisting of a whole range of different activities, mostly led from the front).

e. Kids Alpha (This would probably be most successful with children who have shown some interest in the Christian faith.) In my opinion one of the most strategic features of the Alpha course approach is the fact that people are encouraged to ask questions about anything that they want to. Some children thrive if they too are given this opportunity.

f. Children's cell/house group (In this day and age some parents will have problems allowing their children to go to a meeting in a home. However, this can be overcome to some extent if the home chosen to host the meeting is that of one or more of the children who will be in the group. This has the additional advantage that these children are often keen to invite their peers to something happening in their own home.)

g. Special interest club, e.g. a football club.

h. 'Sidewalk' Sunday School. This idea has proved very successful as part of the ministry of Metro Ministries in Brooklyn, New York, and has spread to many other parts of the world. It is particularly suitable for 'inner city areas' where children play on the street. Metro Ministries have pioneered the idea of having a specially adapted truck, the side of which comes down to make a stage, from which to work, but this is obviously not essential.

3. Specials, e.g. holiday clubs.
These can be very successful and attract lots of children, but in my opinion have limited value if it is then another year before the children have opportunity to attend anything else.

4. Meetings for the whole family.

5. School groups.
Often these need to be seen as engaging in pre-evangelism activities.

Questions to ask before starting any of these
1. WHO?
Who are you aiming to reach? Are you planning to have a mixture of children from church families (who, of course, may not be Christians themselves!) and children from non-Christian homes? What age group are you going to target? (Making this too wide can cause a lot of problems.)

2. WHEN?
Do some research as to what other clubs, etc., happen in the area. Is Saturday morning a better option than a mid-week evening? What programmes are on the TV that children might not want to miss? It is important to make it as easy as possible for them to come, so try not to put them in the position of having to make difficult choices.

3. WHERE?
Location can have an enormous influence on whether something will be successful or not. Is it accessible to the children? Will you offer transportation? Is it the right size? (Too big or too small both have their disadvantages). Is it in good condition? Is it conducive to use by children? Is it possible to have it at the right temperature? (Too hot or too cold can both cause problems.) Should it be on church premises or a building such as a community centre which is more neutral?

4. WHAT?
What kind of advertising are you going to do? Whatever you decide, you need to make it clear that it is a Christian based club otherwise there is the potential of difficulties later. Children themselves are often excellent at spreading the word. Always give a telephone number of a contact person so that parents can call and get information if they want to. If posters are used ensure that they are of a high quality; scruffy-looking posters might give the impression that the club will be substandard.

What kind of programme are you going to have?

What charge, if any, are you going to make for attending the club?

NECESSARY REQUIREMENTS

1. Clear, agreed short-term and long-term vision. (This needs to fit in with the church's whole vision for children's ministry.)

2. Leaders who are committed to the long haul. If the church is struggling to get enough leaders for other children's activities the same problem will probably exist in this situation. It's better not to make a start than have to give up after only a short time because of a lack of leaders.

3. Prayer. Evangelism amongst children is not always easy and it will be necessary to get as much prayer cover as possible.

4. Children who will come. Some schools will be happy to advertise a new club, especially if there is already a good relationship between the church and the school, and it's even better if there are those that go in and do assemblies.

   Children of parents who have attended or who are attending an Alpha course or other adult evangelistic activity should be invited.

   Children who are part of the church family can be great advertisers.

5. A good programme that is thoroughly prepared and has lots of variety.

6. Good discipline. It is vital that good discipline patterns are established from the beginning. Decide and agree on the rules and keep to them. There is a tendency to think that you will drive children away if you are too firm but, if you don't have a good standard of discipline, then everyone will ultimately suffer.

7. Clear presentation of the Gospel ➤ response ➤ discipling. A good follow-up programme is vital.

8. Are children going to be invited to other activities in the church? If the answer is yes, ensure that you have adequate facilities and leaders.

9. Are you going to visit the homes of the children? This can be a good way of showing a greater level of commitment to the children.

FOLLOW-UP

This is absolutely vital if we are going to make 'disciples and not just get decisions'. The aim should always be not just to reach children with the Gospel but to bring them into the Kingdom and to keep them there. There will always be children who will make a response to the Gospel but who won't get involved on an on-going basis in any follow-up work, and it is at these times that we need to trust them to God.

Children who make an initial response to the Gospel need some teaching about the basics of the Faith (e.g. God the Father, God the Son, God the Holy Spirit, the Bible, prayer, worship, witnessing, the church, baptism, communion, the devil, sin and temptation, repentance and forgiveness). These things must be taught in an exciting and dynamic way, so that the children not only grasp these important foundational aspects of Christianity, but also begin to apply the truths that they are learning to their own lives.

Since every situation will be different (numbers of children, leaders, facilities, existing meetings, etc.) there can be no set formula as to the best way to do follow up. Prayer, careful planning and a realistic assessment of each individual situation is essential.

POSSIBLE OPTIONS

1. One to one/two.
One adult could disciple one or two children. This could happen in the context of a meeting either midweek or on Sundays. However, the adult should never take the child to a separate room or out of sight of the main group.

2. Small integrated group.
Establish a group which includes some children who have been Christians for some time and who are perhaps showing some evangelistic or leadership gifting, and some who have only recently become Christians. Encourage the children who have been following the Lord for a while to share what they know with the others.

3. Large integrated group (including small group work).
This would be a larger group, similar in make-up to the one above apart from the size. Because of the numbers there would be the potential to subdivide the group for part of the programme so as to do some foundational teaching with the new Christians.

4. Discipleship group.
This would be a group specifically formed to cater for the needs of newly converted children.

MATERIALS

The selection or production of suitable materials is another key part of follow-up work. *Grow Up!* by Sammy Horner is a useful booklet, as is *Thank You, Jesus*, which is distributed by Children Worldwide, 'Dalesdown', Honeybridge Lane, Dial Post, Horsham, W. Sussex RH13 8NX.

EVANGELISTIC TOOLS

It is important to use anything and everything available to help bring children to faith in Christ.

There are an increasing number of suitable tracts for children. They are often aimed at different age groups so it is important to check that they are appropriate. The wordless book/beads/worm, as outlined in the section on 'Children's Responses to God' (see page 19), are great evangelistic tools.

COMMON MISTAKES

1. Thinking it is possible to try to win children over by doing lots of attractive activities that have little or no spiritual content. The danger with this is that children will be attracted by these, may build good relationships with the leaders but in the end won't have any interest in the Gospel. We need to be very careful about this since lots of time, money and effort can be put into such situations with minimal results. Our focus needs to be on running a programme in which children get excited about God, and also have a good time because we have provided some attractive activities.

2. Having unrealistic expectations of the children.

3. Not exerting sufficient discipline for fear that it will drive the children away.

4. Having the overriding aim of wanting to get children to church on a Sunday. It may well be that church for these children will be, for example, on a Friday evening when they have their club. A person leading a club for unchurched children on a Friday evening shared with me that she has faced a number of adults in the church questioning her as to why the children don't ever come to church. Her response ultimately was to ask these people when was the last time that they went to church on a Friday evening!

5. Using children to reach parents. While there are lots on instances when children are instrumental in bringing their parents either to church or even to a place of faith this should never be the reason why we engage in children's activities. God is concerned with individuals, and children need to be given the opportunity to respond to the Gospel for themselves. They should not be seen as just the means to reach their parents.

OUR RESPONSE

Children's evangelism can often be tough but the Church must look at it seriously. We need to ask God to communicate his heart to us and we need to be prepared to do whatever he asks us to do, even if it is costly. In the book *Streets of Pain* (a later edition is called *Whose Child is it anyway?*) Bill Wilson shares the story of the work that he is doing in the heart of Brooklyn, New York, where at the time of writing this, Metro Ministries is reaching out to approximately 20,000 children every week. His testimony is extremely challenging but a little story he shares puts the whole thing into perspective:

> *Edward Kimball, a shoe shop assistant and a Sunday school teacher in Chicago, loved boys. He spent hours of his free time visiting the young street urchins in Chicago's inner city, trying to win them for Christ. Through him, a young boy named D. L. Moody got saved in 1858. Moody grew up to be a preacher.*
>
> *In 1879 Moody won to the Lord a young man by the name of F. B. Meyer, who also grew up to be a preacher. An avid enthusiast of personal visitation, Meyer won a young man by the name of J. W. Chapman, who in turn grew up to be a preacher and brought the message of Christ to a baseball player named Billy Sunday. As an athlete/evangelist Sunday held a revival in Charlotte, North Carolina, that was so successful that another evangelist by the name of Mordecai Hamm was invited to Charlotte to preach. It was while Hamm was preaching that a teenager named Billy Graham gave his life to Jesus.*
>
> *It all started with the winning of a child to Jesus.*

We will never know what God is going to do with the children with whom we come into contact but, if we never reach out to these children, we will never even give him the chance.

Exercise 1
Find out what your church's strategy for evangelism is. Consider how evangelism amongst children could fit in with this.

Exercise 2
If you were planning to start a midweek club, what factors would you need to consider?

Keeping children safe

The Children's Act, which became law on 14th October 1991, has major implications for those working with children in all contexts including the church. The provisions made by the Act are designed to support and encourage good practice and safety. They are not there to stop or hinder work with children, they are to encourage the best work possible.

The Act covers three main areas:

1. Day-care provision
2. Child welfare
3. Child protection

The area of the church's work that will be most affected by the legislation are groups where under-8s are involved. It means that such groups have to be registered with the local Social Services Department if they last for more than two hours in any one day in non-dwelling premises. In addition, if a holiday club for any age is held for more than six days a year then it must be registered.

The whole idea of the registration is that essential standards of provision are maintained. It is very unlikely that you will not be allowed to run your activity but suggestions may be given for improvements that should be made.

Equal opportunities and racial groups

Local authorities are required by the Act to have regard to different racial groups to which children within their area belong. All children must be treated equally and we must be careful even about some of the analogies that we use in a church setting, e.g. using the colour 'black' to mean bad and 'white' to mean good (in actual fact the Bible describes sin as being like scarlet).

It is imperative that a clear statement of the purpose of any activity is given with any information or registration forms that parents receive. We need to be 'up front' with our Christian beliefs so that the parents of the children that are involved are clear from the outset about the sort of things that their children will be taught.

LEADERS AND HELPERS

Working with children and young people is one of the most important tasks that any church can undertake. Although most of the people that will be involved in this work will, of necessity, be volunteers, it is imperative that the highest possible standards are adhered to. Everything possible must be done to lessen the possibility of putting children in a church's care at risk. Leaders must be selected with extreme care.

Local authorities take the following factors into consideration before they employ children's workers. We would do well to seriously consider them, before appointing people to work with children in a church context.

1. Previous experience of looking after or working with children and/or young people. (A willingness to undertake some training if there is no previous experience.)

2. The ability to provide warm and consistent care.

3. A willingness to respect the background and culture of children and young people in their care.

4. A commitment to treat all children and young people as individuals and with equal concern.

5. Reasonable physical health, mental stability, integrity and flexibility.

Leader to child ratios

'The more the merrier' – the more leaders we can get without overpowering the children the better. However, there are now some legal minimum requirements.

For 0 to 2 years	1:3 (1 leader to every 3 children)
For 2 to 3 years	1:4 (1 leader to every 4 children)

| For 3 to 8 years | 1:8 (1 leader to every 8 children) |
| For 8+ | 1:8 (1 leader to the first 8 children and 1 more for every further 12 children) |

In every situation there should always be at least two adults, one of whom should be female.

A leader should always avoid being isolated with an individual child for too long and should ensure that another leader knows what the situation is.

PREMISES

The County Council, through the Social Services Department, has a statutory duty to keep registers of:

Premises in their area, other than premises wholly or mainly used as private dwellings, where children are received to be looked after for the day, or for part or parts thereof of a duration or aggregate duration of two hours or longer in any one day.

This means that if a church building is used for a group which includes under-8s for more than two hours in a day then the Social Services must be contacted. The premises must also be registered if a club runs for six consecutive days in a year.

The need to register should not cause any concern since the law presumes that registration will be granted unless there are good reasons why it should not be.

There are a number of things that are required by Social Services for day care centres for children under 8. Churches need to look at these so that they can be seen to be making every effort to provide facilities that are as good as possible. These include:

a. Accommodation

b. Cloakroom

c. Quiet/rest area

d. Storage facilities

e. Outdoor play area

f. Toilet accommodation

g. Food preparation/storage

h. Central heating

i. Refuse store

j. Car parking

Details of the above can be obtained from Social Services in your local area.

HEALTH AND SAFETY

The premises will need to meet the Health and Safety requirements in order to safeguard the children. There must be access to a telephone and all leaders should be made aware of the pre-set procedure to be carried out in the event of an emergency.

Health

1. Children with an infectious illness must not attend.

2. No smoking should be permitted at any time.

3. You will need to provide all parents with a form to complete, giving details of any medical needs, contact numbers, etc.

Accidents

1. An accident record book must be kept.

2. Any accidents occurring during a session must be recorded in the Accident Book.

First Aid

1. A simple first aid kit must be kept. The equipment should be stored in a waterproof container, clearly marked as a First Aid Kit.

2. At least one leader must have a recognised first aid training although all leaders should be encouraged to have a knowledge of first aid.

Administering medicines

1. No medication should be administered without written parental consent.

2. A signed record of having administered the medicine must be kept.

3. All medicines must be stored carefully and should be clearly marked with the child's name, dosage and date.

HIV/AIDS

1. Disposable gloves and aprons should be available and gloves should always be worn when dealing with broken skin, body fluids or faeces.

2. Confidentiality of information regarding a child's HIV status must be strictly maintained.

Safety

Due care needs to be given to the following:

1. Fire prevention
2. Cleaning materials
3. Kitchens
4. Badges
5. End of session/Collection of children

CONCLUSION

The above recommendations may seem quite onerous but in a church situation we need to be doing all that we can to ensure that we are beyond reproach in every area. We should see these things as helps rather than hindrances and hang on to the fact that nothing is too good for the children that God has entrusted to us.

Exercise 1

Imagine the following situation:

You are leading the 5-7s group. There are 20 children in the group and one of the children has behavioural problems. You have one helper, a 13-year-old girl.

Five minutes before the end of the session disaster strikes:

Julie is sick.

Your helper, who has only been coming to the church for a month, panics and runs out before she is sick too.

Joshua (the boy with behavioural problems) kicks Megan, who starts to cry.

At the same time Katie drops her felt tip which rolls under the cupboard and she demands your help to get it out.

Sophie is desperate to go to the toilet.

Identify the problems and suggest what could have been done to avoid them.

Movement and dance

Children are active beings and naturally express things with the whole of their being. It is only as they become 'tainted' with adult inhibition that they become more restricted and embarrassed. In movement and dance we are giving opportunity and encouragement for children to recover something of their natural ability.

We are made in the image of God, and the essence of his life is in us. Jesus comes to bring that to life, and we discover something of the nature of God through our emotions. Dance has been described as 'motion that arises out of emotion'. It is ideally total uninhibited abandonment before God, and is for his eyes only. We need to encourage children to understand movement and dance as an act of worship, not a performance, and so, although we want it to be the best we can offer, it does not have to be absolutely right. It is each child's unique expression; no one can give to God what the individual child can give him. And God is thrilled – he likes it!

In movement and dance we need to encourage the use of the body to its fullest extent. It is helpful to give children opportunity to discover what they can express through the use of their bodies – to be in touch with every part – and to bring their bodies under control. They need encouraging to link their movement to their emotions and thoughts, and find ways of communicating these.

It is helpful to impress upon them that they can have their own unique movement 'vocabulary', and to give time to the development of this. This helps to reduce embarrassment and the feeling of not being as good as someone else. Remember it is for God, 'an audience of one'!

PRACTICAL GUIDELINES AND SUGGESTIONS

1. Describe it as movement rather than dance.
Boys and men can often be wary of movement because of the stereotyped impression given of dance. What you call it can make all the difference!

2. Use a man to demonstrate whenever possible.

3. Encourage more strong and sustained movements rather than light and delicate ones.
This helps boys to opt in, and for 'dance' to be more credible. Girls don't miss out – as they are

helped to extend their vocabulary, and they naturally retain the more feminine expressions.

4. In 'free' movement/dance it is not necessary to interpret every part of the song.
Sometimes it is better to interpret the general mood, theme or idea. Also not every part of the song need have movement with it. This is especially true if using banners (flags) or ribbons.

5. Be careful not to 'over use' movement and have every song accompanied by dance.
This is not necessary, and also detracts from the variety and effectiveness. Help the children to be selective and spontaneous.

6. 'Choreographed' songs.
These can sometimes help children in their worship. It involves putting set movements to a song. These need to be demonstrated and explained so that the children understand what they are doing (e.g. in 'You Laid Aside Your Majesty' some difficult language and ideas can be made more accessible to children through the use of movement). It is occasionally valid to choreograph a dance with children that can then be used as a contribution to worship in a way that helps others who are watching. Often, in this context, children will be moving in relation to, and with, others rather than on their own.

7. Incorporate 'signing' with movement.
This can be very effective but don't be too ambitious by trying to interpret every word.

8. Use all levels – high, middle and low.
This increases the vocabulary and creates more interest. Holding positions momentarily before moving on also adds variety.

9. Use passages of Scripture to move or dance to.
These can come alive in a fresh way to participators and audience when they are interpreted through movement and dance (e.g. Creation; Ecclesiastes 3:1-8).

10. Use movement prophetically.
This involves expressing in movement rather than verbally what God might want to reveal or say. Children need some help initially to know that this is possible and to explore ways of doing it.

11. Organise workshops.
Children will greatly benefit from having time when they can learn basic techniques, have some

teaching about the importance of dance and movement, etc.

Children will also need a context in which to operate. This can only be the case if the church encourages dance and movement and acknowledges the importance of it.

BANNERS AND RIBBONS

Children love to use these as an expression of praise and worship.

Simple ribbons can be made with 12-inch split canes and lengths of coloured crepe paper or florist's ribbon, if proper ribbons are not possible. Children do also need a ribbon of appropriate length, especially if they are younger.

Banners can also be made using coloured material and sticks of appropriate length for the children. A good activity is to talk about the use of banners with children, and help them design their own symbols.

Banners are meant to be conspicuous and need to be flaunted. They are a sign or signal meant to distinguish or mark something out. Banners tell people who you represent and indicate past victories. They stir morale and lead people to action. They indicate something to the enemy and can cause them to take flight. Used in praise and worship they are a visual demonstration of spiritual truth, declaring praise to God and victory over the enemy.

Practicalities

a. Try to encourage the use of banners and ribbons only in meetings.
Because children like them so much they will often 'play with them' outside of the meetings. This can devalue their use.

b. Encourage the use of the whole body.
As soon as people get hold of a banner or ribbon and start to use it, they often move only their hand or arm and forget about the rest of their body. They need encouraging to see the banner or ribbon as an extension of themselves, and involve the whole of their body.

c. Don't just 'wave' them.
There is much more scope to using banners and ribbons than simply waving them. While God accepts the offering of 'waving', it often helps the children if they are given a wider vocabulary. It also prevents things becoming boring and predictable.

d. Don't just use them in more up-beat songs or in praise.

e. Use them prophetically.

f. Encourage selectivity so that banners and ribbons are not used all the time.
Children find it more difficult than adults to decide when it is appropriate to use banners and when not. Clearly the use of banners and ribbons is to some extent dependent on the amount and type of space available. It may be that they can only be used on occasions, or by a number of children at one time, or for a selected part of a programme when space has been cleared. This needs to be considered before banners or ribbons are introduced.

Exercise 1

Think of a current song (either a children's song or a song used in adult worship) which could lend itself to movement or dance. Work out a choreographed dance for it.

Exercise 2

Using flags or ribbons, work out a dramatic movement to Isaiah 6:1-8. Think about the colour of the flags and/or ribbons you might use.

Exercise 3

Work out a simple line dance or country dance to accompany a children's song. (Country and Western style lends itself well to this.)

Praise and worship

Man's chief and highest end is to glorify God and fully to enjoy him for ever. (Westminster Larger Catechism, 1647)

Everybody would give mental assent to the vital importance of praise and worship in our own individual lives as well as in church life. However, our actions when we are working with children often do not match up to what we say we believe. Much of what we do in a time of praise and worship is limited to merely 'singing songs'! This is largely a result of wrong conceptions about:

1. WORSHIP

Too often praise and worship is equated with music and singing songs. However, it is much wider and deeper than this.

Romans 12:1 says: 'Offer your bodies as living sacrifices, holy and pleasing to God – which is your spiritual worship.'

True praise and worship is the recognition of the greatness and holiness of God which leads us to offer the whole of our lives to him. Songs/music are only a vehicle to help us.

Graham Kendrick says that worship is:

an encounter with the living, caring, suffering Christ, which will send us out into the world to be more like him.

Gillian Raymond in *Dear God, Can You Wink?* writes:

For me, the word 'praise' conjures up the picture of someone jumping up and down, shouting with excitement and glee. It is often related to a specific incident and to something performed or achieved for which I want to thank God. 'Worship' on the other hand, has a greater solemnity and suggests to my mind the picture of someone down on their knees or on their face, speechless with gratitude and joy because of the person in whose presence they are. It has to do more with God's 'being' than with his 'doing'.

Worship should be:

a. An adventure

b. A spiritual exercise, cf. John 4:24

c. Communication with God

d. Relationship building between the worshipper and God

2. CHILDREN

It is a common belief that children:

a. Cannot be expected to enter fully into praise and worship.
But Psalm 8:2 says: 'From the lips of children and infants (*babies!*) you have ordained praise because of your enemies, to silence the foe and the avenger.' This suggests that God not only expects praise from children but that it also has great spiritual significance.

b. Find worship boring.
Unfortunately this is often true – having been forced to sit through lengthy adult orientated worship times from an early age, their views are already set.

c. Only enjoy up-tempo action songs and do not like the slower worship songs.
While this may be true initially for some, experience has shown us that children grow to enjoy the worship songs more and more as we persevere in their use.

LEADING CHILDREN IN PRAISE AND WORSHIP

1. Create the 'right' environment.
Provide a relaxed atmosphere where children are wanted, respected, loved and taken seriously. Help the children to feel at ease by telling them what is going to happen during a time of worship.

2. Use language which is understandable.
Don't talk down to the children, but keep your language simple. Be prepared to make adequate explanation of any unfamiliar words contained in songs, readings, etc.

3. Encourage participation.
Give specific instructions, i.e. when to clap, when to pray, when to listen to God, when to share, etc. Draw the children in by speaking over the singing to explain words or encourage participation.

Encourage movement/actions to the songs where appropriate. (See section on Movement and Dance, page 78, for ideas).

4. Remember concentration spans.
Several short bursts are better than one long one!

5. Be a good role model.
Be a worshipper yourself. Remember: never expect a child to do something which you could not or would not do yourself.

6. Encourage a variety of expressions of worship.
For example, thanking, praising, shouting, clapping, dancing, lifting hands, kneeling, leaping, etc.

7. Don't be afraid to exert discipline.

8. Include times to listen to God.
Expect God to speak out of the worship. Children need to experience this two-way communication and so times for listening to God need to be built into the programme.

9. Plan the worship time.
Decide where you think the focus ought to be. The worship and response time needs as much planning as the Bible teaching! It's your job to lead the children into the presence of God.

10. Choose suitable songs.
Have a good balance of praise and worship songs in every meeting. It's good sometimes to allow the children to choose their favourite songs, but generally speaking the choice should lie with you. Choose some songs with actions that will help participation.

TAKING A CLOSER LOOK AT SONGS

It's important to take a good look at songs. Some words are just right, but the tune can be dreary or complicated and vice versa. Both are important because music becomes the vehicle which enables us to enter into the words and really mean them. On the other hand, music can just give us an aesthetic, sentimental or enjoyable feeling and the words are lost.

Praise and worship songs can be *about* God or directed *to* God. The majority of hymns, for example, are *about* God, praising him and extolling his greatness, etc., while many slower worship songs are sung *to* God, saying how we feel about him and offering our lives to him. Again, both have a part to play, although sadly, many of us neglect the latter.

We need to use a wide variety of songs with different aims in mind:

1. Songs of rejoicing, thanksgiving, praise and exhortation.
These types of songs are often best used at the very start of a meeting and often their focus is manward rather than Godward. ('Come on, everybody, let's join together and sing . . .', 'We're the kids of the King', 'Let's celebrate'.)

2. Songs of worship.
('Love you, Jesus, I love you, Lord . . .', 'Worship the King'.)

3. Songs for response/ministry.
('Come, Jesus, come, touch my heart with a deep compassion . . .', 'Lord, look into my heart'.)

4. Songs to teach Scripture verses.

5. Songs/music for dance, drama and mime.

6. Prophetic songs.
('Jesus says, keep close . . .')
These need not necessarily be new, spontaneous songs but any that contain an element of God speaking in a direct way to the children. This type of song will often come out of a time of listening to God.

7. Adult songs.
There are an increasing number of songs written for adults that are also accessible to children. Songs which include an echo (e.g. 'I will worship, I will worship . . .') work well with children since they just have to follow the leader rather than read a lot for themselves. I have found songs like 'My Jesus, my Saviour' to be very popular with children, and even children who cannot read all the words generally manage to focus on the 'Shout to the Lord' phrase, listening and waiting to join in at that point. Some of the simple worship songs that have come out of the Vineyard movement are also very suitable.

Generally it is good to try and use some of the songs used in adult worship in children's groups. Once the children are familiar with these songs and confident with them they will be more inclined to join in if they hear them in a situation which is not specifically geared to them.

The songs mentioned in this section are from cassettes recorded by Powerpack which are available from The Powerpack Trust, 21A, Mountside, Guildford, Surrey GU2 5JD.

N.B. Try not to use songs as 'fillers' in the programme since it has the effect of devaluing true worship.

WRITE YOUR OWN!

Why not try to write your own songs? Start by taking a Scripture verse or write words of your own. Then add a simple tune. If this is too hard then get together with someone else who has this particular ability and work on it together. You'll be surprised what you can do!

Some simple tips for writing children's songs:

- Keep words and tune fairly simple, especially for younger children.
- Make songs shorter rather than longer.
- Think about the relevance of the words for the age group for whom you are writing.
- Words can reflect and encourage specific expressions of worship, e.g. lifting hands, shouting, clapping, etc.
- Musical interludes can allow for times of free dancing or quiet reflection.
- Unless you are a well-accomplished musician keep the accompaniment fairly simple. It can be difficult to lead the children in praise and worship and follow a complicated score!
- Use synth sounds as backing, special effects, whistles, etc. A drum machine can be useful in composing a rap.

HELP! I CAN'T DO IT!

1. It's not me!

Little is said or taught about the different giftings needed within the whole area of children's work. So, more often than not, children's leaders are required to be able to do everything, especially if they are the only one with a group of children! Hence a leader may try to lead praise and worship knowing they have little or no gifting in this area, which may leave them feeling insecure or inadequate. Alternatively they may not even attempt it.

Antidotes:
a. Ask God for a special anointing for these times.

b. Follow the guidelines for leading worship laid out above.

c. If all fails find someone to help you, even if it's just for the time of praise and worship.

2. We don't have a musician!

Well, all is not lost! You don't have to be a musician to lead worship! While it is obviously better to have a resident musician there are ways round it!

Antidotes:
a. 'Import' a musician who does not have to be a children's worker.
Remember, you will still need to plan and lead the worship yourself. Often this will mean that the praise and worship time can only be one block in your programme.

b. Use CDs/cassettes.
Fade out songs that you feel may be too long. Some recordings now include a split track facility giving the option of singing with backing tracks. CDs are easier to work with than cassettes but many children's praise and worship albums are still only available on cassette.

c. Learn to play an instrument yourself.
That's how many an excellent guitarist has started!

d. Use musically gifted children.
Many children may like to play for worship but there does need to be a fair degree of proficiency or the worship will suffer and so will you! Encourage others to learn. Explore the possibility of forming a children's worship band! Preparation will be essential for this, and finding a time to practise will be necessary.

N.B. The playing of instruments often means that the children involved do not enter into worship, so be prepared to release them to respond.

e. Prepare praise and worship which does not involve singing.

1. Write a Psalm. Give the children a starting line and go from there.

2. Write a rap together in praise of God. Use a drum machine/synth as backing.

3. Write a letter to God. Encourage the children to tell him how they feel. (You may need to do the writing!)

4. Write a prayer of praise in the form of an acrostic, e.g. 'PRAISE GOD'. Tell the children to think about what God is like and write a sentence containing each letter reflecting their thoughts; e.g. God you are **P**owerful.

5. Give the children verses to look up relating to a characteristic of God. Discuss them and then use them as a basis for praise and worship.

6. 'Praise consequences'. A child writes down on paper WHO God is – then passes the paper on to the next child who writes WHAT God does and so on, answering the questions Who, What, Where.

7. Listen to different excerpts of music. Ask the children what characteristics of God the music reminds them of.

8. Responsive reading. The leader reads out truths about God and the children respond to each by saying 'IT'S TRUE' or 'THIS IS OUR GOD', etc.

9. Finish the Sentence! The leader says something like 'God, only you could . . .' and all of the children take turns to complete the sentence. The leader writes down all the answers and then the children choose which ones they like best and record them on cassette. This can then be replayed and used as part of a praise time.

10. Children make up a Praise Game, in the style of 'snakes and ladders'. Squares could read 'Forgot to thank God. Go back 3', 'Praise God for loving me. Shake again', etc. Then the children can play the game and use some of the positive statements in a praise time.

11. Make a poster. Children draw or cut out magazine pictures of things they could praise and thank God for. These can then be used as a basis for prayer and praise.

12. Alphabet praise. Find a word that can be used to praise God starting with each letter of the alphabet.

N.B. Many of these suggestions are prayer activities also.

3. My kids won't sing!

Sometimes, especially with older children, singing can become more of a hindrance to worship than a help. Where groups are small the children can feel embarrassed or feel that it's just not 'cool'! In these cases why struggle? Use some of the ways mentioned above instead.

4. I've no OHP!

Some facilities do not allow for an OHP. In these cases why not write words out on sheets of card or make up a songsheet for your group? Both, of course, have limitations.

5. We can't make any noise!

Often rooms need to be shared with other groups, or are in too close proximity and then there is the problem of disturbance. It may be that in the main you will need to use the methods outlined above in Section 2. However, you could try joining together for a period of time.

FINALLY, IT IS IMPORTANT TO REMEMBER THAT YOU CANNOT TAKE THE CHILDREN FURTHER THAN YOU HAVE GONE YOURSELF. WE NEED CONSTANTLY TO BE AT THE VERY LIMIT OF WHAT WE CAN COPE WITH OURSELVES!

Exercise 1

Look through the Psalms and make a list of all the different expressions of praise and worship that you can find.

Exercise 2

Below is an example of a possible one-hour programme for 7-11 year olds with the theme 'Be Strong and Courageous' as mentioned on The Balanced Programme notes (see page 17). Choose songs and other activities for the praise and worship/ministry sections.

11:00	Praise
11:05	Teaching – Bible Base Daniel 1
11:15	Memory Verse Joshua 1:9
11:25	Drama – All Together (Joshua)
11:35	Puppets (Don't Be Afraid)
11:40	Worship/Ministry
11:50	Quiz
11:58	Prayer/Closing Song

Prayer

Children are excited about praying. Change the world – that's what praying children do. Teach and train them NOW! (Rev William Ilnisky, Pastor, Assemblies of God, USA)

In these days there is much talk about and encouragement to engage in prayer, particularly for God to move in power and to bring revival. Many believe that children need to be involved in this renewed emphasis on prayer, and leaders, parents, etc., need to be doing all that they can to help them be participators rather than just observers.

However, in my experience, the most frequent comment from children's leaders is, 'My children just won't pray, it is like getting blood out of a stone!' This is a far cry from what God wants and from what we hear is happening in some parts of the world. I believe that God has to do something sovereignly to change the hearts of children and to excite them about prayer but there are things that we can do to facilitate this. Children need training in and teaching about prayer, they need to see how they can be involved and how important it is that they start to participate in an effective way. They need to understand that:

Prayer is contact with God, bringing us into touch with him day by day, moment by moment, as we learn to communicate with him and allow him to communicate with us. (Gillian Raymond in *Dear God, can you wink?*)

PRAYER – THE BASICS

1. Prayer should first and foremost be an adventure as we talk to God and build our relationship with him. Children need to be encouraged to just 'chat' with God in a natural way about the ordinary everyday occurrences of their lives, before ever asking him for anything.

    Jesus, can you listen now, please? I need to whisper 'cos Mum's here. Thank you that Leon sanded down the roofing iron today and washed it ready for painting. I loved standing under the dirty water when he stood on the roof and squirted the hose and all the mess waterfalled off the gutter. It was good even though Mummy got mad that I was soaked and I got all that rust in my clothes and in my hair. Amen (Gillian Raymond in *Dear God, can you wink?*).

2. We need to help create the desire to pray in children, they should want to pray.

3. What children learn about prayer when they are young will have an effect on their patterns of prayer throughout their lives. They need to grow up thinking that prayer is a natural part of life.

4. A child will learn to pray by seeing others pray and by seeing the way in which they expect a response, talk about and act upon the answers they get.

5. Prayer on a Sunday will be all the more real to a child if he has already assimilated something of what prayer is all about at home.

6. The amount of time that we give to prayer will often reflect how important we regard it.

7. Children and long prayers don't usually mix!

8. We need to create the right environment for prayer to happen, e.g. encourage the children to pray at specific times about specific things.

9. Language used in prayer needs to be carefully considered.

10. Children need to see that prayer 'works'. It is important that they are told about answers to prayer.

11. Children will expect immediate answers to their prayers; we must not squash their faith but on the other hand we must make them aware of the fact that God may answer with a yes, a no, or a wait.

12. Children need to be helped to stand back from situations that they are praying for, and look at them from God's perspective. This is foundational to the development of intercessory prayer.

13. Children are naturally open, trusting and honest. This should be reflected in the way they pray.

14. It is good to encourage children to develop routines of prayer but they should never become rigid, religious exercises!

15. Most children start their prayers 'Dear Lord Jesus . . .' This is probably because we have modelled this with them. We need to help children develop a wider concept of the God to whom they are praying, by encouraging them to address all three persons of the Trinity depending on the content of their praying.

LISTENING TO GOD

We do not just make conversation 'at' God, because the word 'conversation' implies that he does his share of the talking too. We need to be alert constantly, listening, so that whenever he has something to say to us, he simply has to catch our attention and go ahead. (Gillian Raymond)

Children need to be trained to listen 'to' God, i.e. to hear and to obey all that he says, and in order to do this they must learn how to listen out 'for' God.

Children need:

a. to be taught about the different ways in which God speaks.

b. to practise listening to God.

c. to be helped to take what God says seriously and act on it.

d. to be told to leave spaces when they talk to God so that he can answer.

Leaders need:

a. to be good listeners to God themselves.

b. to leave time in the course of a meeting for 'true conversational prayer'.

c. to be prepared to clarify for the children what God says.

d. to take what God says and apply it in a way that the children can respond to.

e. to help the children relax and not to 'stress and strain' to hear God.

f. to allow children to use natural, everyday language. Discourage religious jargon!

GETTING STARTED

Chris and John Leach in their book, *And For Your Children*, recommend a five-step programme to help children to pray out loud. This can work for children of all ages but may take more time if the children are younger.

Step 1: Leader does everything – chooses a prayer subject, prays about it and says Amen at the end. Subjects need to be simple and relevant (possibly linked with the teaching). The leader models short jargon-free prayers. Eventually the children join in with the Amen.

Step 2: Children repeat prayers phrase by phrase after the leader.

Step 3: Children are asked to suggest items for prayer, then back to step two.

Step 4: Children suggest items for prayer and the leader suggests how they might pray. This could be a set formula like 'Dear Lord Jesus, please look after _____ this week. Amen'

Step 5: Children think of an issue, compose a prayer and say it out loud.

DEVOTIONAL PRAYER

The majority of the ideas above are aimed at encouraging children in some form of intercessory prayer but it is also vitally important that children are helped to develop a devotional prayer life.

Children will need to be encouraged to:

1. Schedule a time when they can be alone with the Lord.

2. Find a suitable place where they will not be disturbed and where it is as easy as possible for them to concentrate.

3. Persevere when they don't feel that they are 'connecting' with the Lord.

4. Develop a rounded prayer time including:

a. Prayer
b. Worship
c. Meditation
d. Speaking in tongues
e. Silence

5. Develop a 'devotional' vocabulary. The following could be helpful:

a. Make a list of words to describe God/Jesus

b. Make a list of praise words

c. Take a couple of verses from one of the devotional Psalms, e.g. Ps. 3, 7, 8, 9, 23, 24, 34, 42, 51, 63, 84, 89, 91, 103, 104, 111, 138, 139 and use them as a basis for prayer.

d. Listen to a worship song and use the words of songs as a basis of prayer

e. Use the Lord's prayer as a framework for prayer

f. Make a list of all the things for which God can be thanked. Use the list as a basis for thanksgiving in future times of prayer.

6. Realise that prayer takes effort and that they should not feel condemned if they fail. Instead they should just start again and ask God to help them persevere.

CONCLUSION

Sadly, many of us live with crippled prayer-lives: the more we can do to save future generations from this fate by training them into good habits early, the better for them and for the kingdom of God. (Chris and John Leach in *And For Your Children*)

THE ONLY WAY TO LEARN HOW TO PRAY IS TO ACTUALLY PRAY

It has been documented in the history of revivals, that when children begin to pray, revival is hastened. (Gary Bergel, *Intercessors for America*)

Exercise 1
Make a list of answers to prayer that you have had in your life. Are there any of these that you can share with the children?

Exercise 2
Consider starting a prayer meeting or planning a prayer section as part of your programme. What factors need to be borne in mind in an attempt to make this both successful and effective?

Prayer activities

It is important that children don't have the idea that prayer and fun can't go together. The activities below are suitable for a variety of ages and situations. Always try something out before doing it with children and make sure that any materials that are prepared are of a good standard.

1. Teaspoon

tsp = thank you, sorry, please

NB: There needs to be some teaching on what it means to be sorry, or in biblical terms, to repent. The word sorry implies two things: 'I wish I hadn't done that' and 'I won't do it again'.

2. Acts

Adoration, **C**onfession, **T**hanksgiving, **S**upplication.

This mnemonic is a good basis for teaching about and practising the different aspects of prayer.

3. Prayer pictures or posters

Children draw a picture or poster around a prayer theme, e.g. 'God we think you are . . .' Display the pictures and use the ideas as a basis for a prayer time.

4. Prayer hand

Start with the thumb, work round the fingers for praise, confession, thanksgiving, asking for others, asking for ourselves.

5. Praying God's word

Choose a verse of Scripture for each child. Get them to think about it and use it as a basis for a prayer. For example, Psalm 23:1, 'The Lord is my Shepherd, I shall lack nothing'. A possible prayer could be something along the lines of, 'Father, thank you that you look after me and give me everything I need.'

6. Pass-it-on prayer

a. Children each pray round in a circle. One child starts the prayer, the next carries it on, the last child finishes it off.

b. Pass an object, e.g. a Bible, round a circle. When a child has the Bible then it is their turn to pray. (Perhaps the use of music as in the traditional party game would add the dimension of children not knowing who will be next.)

N.B. The children may need to be helped with ideas, etc., before you start and care is needed not to 'push' those who are still not ready to participate in this way.

7. Prayer alphabet poster

Make a poster with the letters of the alphabet. Every time you meet, ask the children to suggest things to pray for beginning with one of the letters, and write it in the correct place. Use the poster as a basis for the prayer time. (This is particularly suitable for younger children.)

8. Thanks banks

Each child makes a box with a slit in the top (like a money box). During the week they write things that they can thank God for on small pieces of paper and 'deposit' them in their 'bank'. When they meet together they can open their 'banks', share what God has done and then thank God together.

9. Prayer charts

Either give each child a chart (or if they are able, let them make their own). This should be in grid form like a calendar showing a week or a month. The children colour in the appropriate square or use a sticker to indicate the days on which they remember to pray.

10. Prayer books/lists

Sometimes it is good to keep a record of prayer requests and the answers received. This could be in a book, an ordinary list or something more pictorial like leaves on a tree or even balloons! (Pop them when the answer comes.)

11. Prayer concerts

Divide the children into small groups (2-4 max). Give them a short time (e.g. 2 minutes) to pray about a given topic. At the end of that time they regroup and start the process over again with another topic. (Three or four times is probably enough.)

12. Prayer pockets

Make a 'pocket' for each child. (This could be an envelope with the child's name clearly written on the front.) Stick these on to a large sheet of card. When the children arrive they are given small pieces of paper on which to write any prayer requests. These are then placed randomly into the pockets. At some point during the session the children take out the paper in their envelope and pray accordingly.

13. Prayer walking

Take small groups of children out for a walk. Stop at key places and ask the children to pray about that place/object, e.g. a school, hospital, etc. (This could be a time for the children to listen to God or you may need to suggest things they can pray about.)

N.B. If it is not possible to go for an actual walk, use video clips, a map or pictures/newspaper cuttings, etc., displayed around the room to stimulate prayer.

14. Treasure hunt

Working in twos or threes, the children solve clues which take them to various locations where there will be suggestions for prayer. Each stage of the 'hunt' could be timed and a whistle blown as a sign to move on.

15. Prayer pin!

Display a map of your local area, the world, Britain, etc. Blindfold a child, who then places a pin in the map (like 'Pin the tail on the donkey'). The children then pray for that place.

16. Telephone

Encourage very young children to talk to God on a toy telephone.

17. Prayer game

Prepare a 'board game' to be used with a dice and counters. Squares need to be labelled with topics for prayer and different incentives, e.g.
• Prayed for a friend – throw again
• Forgot to pray – go back two spaces

18. A prayer diary

Encourage the children to keep a diary, in writing or picture form, of the things that happen (both good and bad) during the day/week and to use it as a basis of 'chatting to God' as they share their lives with him. This could happen at home as individuals or in a group.

19. Prayer tools

Globall – a soft, huggable ball with a world map on it. It is thrown to a child and while hugging it they have to pray. (It is best to give the child a subject to pray about.)

Prayer spinner – this has different categories for prayer on it. The children spin it and then pray about the subject that the pointer lands on.

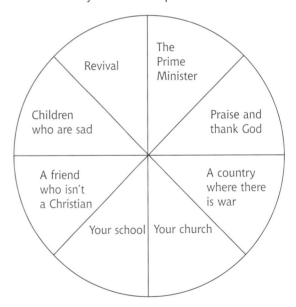

Impression ball – like a 'stress ball' but with a world map on. It is thrown to a child, who is given a subject to pray about as they squeeze the ball. This is a symbolic action showing that they can make an impression on the world.

(All the above are produced by Esther Network International, 854 Conniston Road, West Palm Beach, Florida 33405-2131, USA. Tel: 407-832-6490 Fax: 407-832-8043 [Try making your own prayer spinner.])

Inflatable globe – these are available to buy up to a size of approximately 75cm in diameter. Use it in a similar way to the *Globall* above.

20. Flags

Make some flags (computer clip art is usually a good source of these) of various countries that you want to target in prayer. Stick them around the room and encourage the children to go and stand by the one representing the country for which they are going to pray. Alternatively make them so that they can be held like real flags.

21. Floor

Make some giant floor maps. Spread them round the room. The children stand on them as they pray.

22. Prayer mobile

Each child needs five card shapes which represent different areas of prayer.

A red heart = Thanksgiving and praise to God.

A house shape = Others. Draw or write the names of those whom they will pray for regularly especially family members.

An ear = Listening. To remind them to listen to God and that prayer is two-way.

A man = Evangelism. Write the names of two friends, who are not Christians, that they will pray for.

A mirror = Their own needs (stick silver paper/ tin foil on to card to make a mirror).

The children then need two sticks (or even a wire coat hanger will do), and some thread which they can fix on to the shapes with sellotape and tie on to the sticks.

23. Lord's Prayer chain

Divide the Lord's Prayer into short phrases. Write these on to strips of paper all of the same colour (or buy 'paper chains'). Then cut more strips of different colours. Ask the children to suggest, and, if they can, write on these, words which amplify or further describe each phrase. Make up the chain by sequencing phrase followed by description, etc. This is probably best done over a number of sessions.

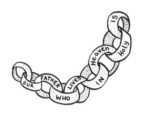

24. Prayer banners

Make some banners out of fabric or paper/card. (The children could be involved in this.) Each banner needs to represent a different subject for prayer. The number used at any one time needs to reflect the number of children in the group. Position them around the room and tell the children to go and stand in front of the one depicting the subject about which they are going to pray. Some pointers as to specifics for prayer for each banner need to be given, especially for younger children.

More ideas can be found in the Powerpack training pack entitled 'Training Up Prayer Warriors' available from the Powerpack Trust, 21A Mountside, Guildford, Surrey, GU2 4JD.

Puppets

Puppets have enormous value for effective communication. Used within the context of a balanced programme they appeal to all ages. They can be used to initiate or to reinforce a point, portraying real life situations. Children readily identify with the puppets and may well talk to a puppet when they would not talk to an adult, thereby also making them a useful tool in difficult counselling situations.

A child's concentration span is said to be approximately one minute per year of their age (that is at an optimum level), but experience has shown that this can be extended by the use of puppets mainly because they are such a visual means of communication.

Another advantage of using puppets is that just a minimum of props is required, while the only major disadvantage is the limited number of movements possible.

THE USE OF PUPPETS

A puppet theatre is traditionally associated with 'puppet shows' but is not a necessity and in fact can limit movement. Puppets can be used in a variety of ways, either on their own or with drama. They can speak in one of three ways:

1. The puppet pretends to talk to the operator (whispers in his/her ear), i.e. the operator interacts with the puppet.

2. The operator interacts with the puppet and is the voice of the puppet.

3. The operator can be just the manipulator and voice of the puppet, and the puppets can interact with one another.

Practical tips

1. Hold the puppet quite high so that it can be seen easily.

2. Be careful not to block the audience's view of the puppet. Stand behind it rather than at the side.

3. Don't worry if your lips move – there's no need to be a ventriloquist! The children will be far more interested in the puppet than in you!

4. Practise in front of a mirror before using a puppet. Remember to move the puppet's mouth as you speak!

5. Practise portraying different emotional states with your puppet, e.g.
   - Shyness – bring puppet in close to your body, hiding its face.
   - Happiness – move the puppet around in a carefree manner.
   - Fear – make the puppet tremble.
   - Anger – hold the puppet away from your body.
   - Sadness – drop the head of the puppet.
   - Surprise – open the puppet's mouth wide and hold away from your body.

6. Decide on a name and character for your puppet and keep to it. A change in name and character can cause confusion and an inability to identify.

7. Be careful to talk puppet to puppet rather than operator to operator.

8. Always learn the script if you can.

9. Choose puppets that are appropriate to the size of your group, e.g. small hand puppets are ideal for a small group of children but unsuitable for a family service in church or large meeting because of visibility. You can even use ordinary soft toys without a glove or an open mouth – especially with very young children.

DIFFERENT KINDS OF PUPPETS

There are numerous types of puppets ranging from the very simple to the complex. The following list is by no means exhaustive but does include some of the most popular. A puppet theatre may be necessary when working with some types of puppets.

Hand puppets
These are large puppets which are probably the most popular and widely used. They are often used with a puppet theatre.

Glove puppets
These are smaller puppets which can be traditional 'Sooty and Sweep' type puppets or literally can be made out of an old glove, sock or paper bag.

Rod puppets
These are rods with cut-out card figures attached. Movement is limited and a screen is needed.

Shadow puppets
These are nothing more than rod puppets with no surface decoration. The use of a lighted screen adds another dimension to these which compensates for the lack of movement.

Finger puppets
Made of narrow cones of card, material or can be knitted.

Marionettes/string puppets
These are both difficult to make and to operate and do require a puppet theatre if possible.

Pop-up puppets
These are a form of rod puppet which 'pop up' from a fabric covered cone.

Egg box puppets
A cardboard egg box can be used for the head and a cloth body can be attached.

WRITING YOUR OWN SKETCHES
Points to remember:

1. The simpler the better.

2. Choose one point to communicate.

3. Ensure that you choose to portray a situation that is relevant to the age group with which you are working.

4. Watch your language!

5. Be shorter rather than longer.

6. Lots of short speeches are best with as much interaction as possible between the puppets.

7. Introduce humour if possible.

8. Don't try to explain everything in the sketch. You can pick this up later in the programme.

9. Use existing material and adapt it.

CONCLUSION
You don't have to have a massive amount of ability in order to use puppets with children, the important thing is that you 'have a go' and improvement in technique, etc., will develop with practice.

Exercise 1
Practise showing the following emotional states with your puppet.

Anger
Sadness
Fear
Surprise
Happiness
Shyness

Exercise 2
Below is a list of exclamations. Practise using your puppet to say these in the way suggested.

I'm tired!	In an angry way.
I'm fed-up!	In a sad way.
No! I don't want to	In a frightened way.
Why?	In a proud way.
What are you doing?	In a bored way.
It wasn't me!	In an offended way.

Exercise 3
Write a short puppet sketch on the theme of forgiveness. Here is the background:

A has taken something belonging to B without asking permission. The object gets spoiled in some way. B discovers that A has borrowed the object and challenges A about it. Decide the outcome. Will A be forgiven or not?

Remember to think as a child would. What object would be relevant? What could happen to it? What will be A's response? To deny or to confess? It's up to you!

Quizzes

Children really enjoy quizzes and they are a good way of both reinforcing Bible teaching and of finding out how much the children have understood and remembered.

GENERAL POINTS

1. Ensure that the children know the rules before you start, e.g. that they have to raise their hand and wait to be asked before they answer a question. Quizzes can be potential discipline problem points.

2. Divide the children fairly into teams considering age and ability, etc.

3. Be careful that you don't keep asking the same child for the answer.

4. Ask questions on the material that you have taught in that particular session. If things have been added to the story that are not biblical, do not reinforce these by asking questions on them.

5. Be scrupulously fair. Decide beforehand how many chances you are going to give to answer a question and always stick to that.

6. Ensure that children understand the scoring system.

7. Keep the questions fairly short.

8. Use a variety of scoring methods.

9. Write your questions down and keep them for future use.

There are two ways of looking at a quiz, either you just ask questions as a sort of test or you use it as a way in to playing a game, using one of the following scoring methods.

METHODS OF SCORING

1. Dice

2. Numbered spinning wheel

3. Straws containing pieces of paper with numbers on them.

4. Fabric sheet with numbered holes through which a ball or bean bag is thrown.

5. Numbered containers into which balls are thrown.

6. Bag with folded pieces of paper each with a different number.

7. 'Pointer' (in the style of 'Pin the tail on the donkey'). The child is blindfolded and points to a numbered score sheet.

8. Darts.

9. Skittles (these can be proper skittles or home-made ones using tins, bottles).

The above is not exhaustive; try thinking of original ideas of your own. Remember 'variety is the spice of life'!

RECORDING THE NUMBERS

Ladders

Each team has their own ladder and small character figure/counter. The winner is the first to get to the top. The ladders can be drawn on card or an OHP sheet.

Scoreboard

Make a board on which to hang numbers up to 100 or use a flip-over number system.

Snakes and ladders

Use a giant version of this popular board game or other similar game.

Faces

Like a game of beetle. Draw a face shape for

each team, choose a scoring method and fill in the features as follows: 1=mouth, 2=nose, 3=eyes, 4=ears, 5=hair, 6=eyebrows. The winner is the first to complete their face or get the most features.

Dotto/boxes

Draw a grid of dots, say 8 x 8. The children draw in the number of lines that they score using one of the above scoring methods, creating as many boxes as possible. The team with the highest number of completed boxes is the winner. (Alternatively, using different colours to represent each team, the children must create boxes only of their own colour.)

TYPES OF QUESTIONS

Depending on the type of quiz, questions will either be based on the teaching or of a general nature. If general, make them more interesting by using different kinds, for example, Bible sums, True or false?, Occupations, Newspaper headlines, How many?, Odd man out, Who am I?, Old Testament/New Testament.

Quiz games

Below is a list of tried and tested quiz games. These have been particularly enjoyed by 9-13 year olds. The quiz questions need to be of a general nature and within the knowledge of most of the children. To personally make your own book of such questions is very useful, although initially quite time consuming.

Many of the games below will involve the use of gameboards and/or scorecards. These can be made from strong card covered with contact or laminated so that they are reusable.

Instructions have been given for all the games though many of them may be well known.

1. Noughts and crosses

Equipment
Draw out the noughts and crosses grid on a whiteboard or chalkboard or make a gameboard and Os and Xs cards as illustrated.

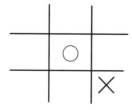

How to play
Divide the children into two teams, one being noughts and the other crosses. Each team earns the right to place a nought or cross in one of the sections of the grid after answering a quiz question correctly. The first team to make a line, horizontally, vertically or diagonally is the winner.

This game may be varied by allocating categories, e.g. Women in the Bible, Kings and Queens, etc., to each section of the grid – perhaps making the centre square questions a little harder.

An alternative is to play 'human' noughts and crosses, where the children themselves are the Os or Xs and place themselves in the sections of a grid previously marked out on the floor.

2. Blockbuster

Equipment
A gameboard with a lettered 'honeycomb' grid – five hexagons across and four down (see diagram), two sets of different coloured hexagon markers

and sets of questions whose answers begin with A, B, C, etc. (You will need quite a few for each letter.)

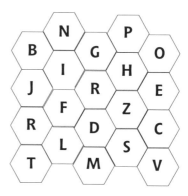

How to play
Divide children into two teams and number them. The idea of the game is to connect a 'run' of letters either across or down the board. One team will play across, the other down. Decide who will go first by asking a 'free for all' question. The team to start decides whether to go down or across and chooses a letter from the grid. A question (whose answer will begin with that letter) is asked to the number one in that team. If the answer is correct then the hexagon is covered with one of the team's coloured markers. Another letter is then chosen by the team and number two is asked the next question and so on until an answer is not known or is incorrect. Then the opposing number in the other team is offered the question. If answered correctly the game moves to the other team and so on. The winning team is the one to reach the opposite side of the grid whether across or down.

3. Bible mimes

The game is basically a game of charades. Divide the children into two or more teams and a child from each team reports to the leader who gives them a Bible story or character to mime for the other members of their team to guess. The child who guesses the story or character then goes to the leader for a further mime.

4. Twenty questions

Select a few articles or people from the Bible and divide the children into two teams. By asking a maximum of twenty questions, whose answers can only be yes or no, each team takes turns in guessing what the article or who the person may be.

5. Treasure island

Equipment
Draw out a map of an island, labelling various places where buried treasure could be found, e.g. Shark Bay, Crocodile Swamp, Snake Wood, etc. Also write the names of these places on small pieces of card.

How to play
At the start of the game the leader selects one of the cards (unseen) from the set. This is the location of the treasure for that game. Divide the children into two teams asking questions alternately. A correct answer gives the team the opportunity of guessing where the treasure is. The winning team is obviously the one who finds the treasure first.

6. Cricket

Equipment
A gameboard (as in diagram) and non-permanent OHP marker. (This board will need laminating or covering with contact as it needs to be written on.) A list of 10 questions for each team will also be required. Unknown to the children, the leader randomly allocates 'runs' to both sets of questions, making sure the total is the same. One question in each set will earn six runs, two will earn four runs, two will earn three runs, two will earn two runs and three will earn one run. The same number question for each team should not carry the same number of runs.

TEAM 1	TEAM 2
1 2 3 4 5 6 7 8 9 10	1 2 3 4 5 6 7 8 9 10

How to play
Divide the children into two teams. Decide who will 'bowl' first and who will 'bat'. The 'bowlers' choose a number question for the 'batters' and if the answer is correct the 'batters' will score the number of runs previously allocated to that question. The teams take it in turns to alternately 'bat' and 'bowl' after each question. The first team to get 20 runs wins. It is also possible to allocate 'wickets' to one or two of the questions which then act as forfeits and the 'batters' are bowled out and have the runs deducted instead of added!

7. Pictionary

This is a very popular game. Divide the children into two or more teams. A child from each team reports to the leader who gives them a biblical character, place, article which they must draw for their team to guess. The first team to complete all the selected items wins the game.

8. Misreads

Equipment
Well-known Bible story, two different sounding squeaky toys.

How to play
Divide into two teams, seated around squeaky toy. Read a well-known Bible story correctly telling the children to be very careful to listen to every detail. Then reread the story substituting mistakes, e.g. instead of 'Zacchaeus was a tax collector' you might read 'Zacchaeus was a taxi driver!' The children have to spot the mistakes and the first team to squeak their toy wins a point and the opportunity to earn a further point if they can correct the mistake. This could be passed to the other team if the correct answer is not known. Should a team squeak the toy when there has not been a misread they forfeit a point.

9. It's in the bag!

Equipment
A bag or box containing various objects which speak of a story, an incident or a character in the Bible.

How to play
Divide into two teams. Take turns in taking out an object without looking and associating a Bible incident, story or character to it. Alternatively,

each team could see who could find the most associations.

10. Matching pairs

Equipment

Sets of identical cards (2s or 4s) of Bible characters, etc. (pictures for younger children, words for older), or sets of associated characters or situations, e.g. Daniel/Lions, Mary/Joseph, etc.

How to play

Divide into two teams, arrange cards face down and take turns to find matching pairs, turning over and replacing each time if there is not a match. The team with the most pairs is the winner.

11. Outburst

Equipment

Scorecard from say 1 to 50, counters to move along the scorecard, a set of cards each with a list of 10 names or things of different categories, numbered 1-10, e.g. 10 women in the Bible, 10 animals mentioned in the Bible, 10 foods, etc., 10 cities, and so on (these must be covered with contact or laminated). You will also need a non-permanent OHP marker and an egg timer or stop watch.

How to play

Divide into two (or more) teams. Decide who will go first. The leader takes a card from the top of the pile, reads the category, and sets the egg timer or stop watch going (1 min). The team has to call out as many possible answers as they can in the time. Points can only be scored for answers which appear on the card even though there may be other possibilities – one point for each correct answer. When the time is up the points are recorded on the scorecard and the other team has a turn.

N.B. This is a simplified version of the secular game with which you may be familiar. If you want to make it a little more interesting then each team could also be given three tokens. If they do not like the category on their card they can surrender a token and be allocated another (this can happen only three times). Also, you could make two sets of different coloured cards, one with numbers 1 to 10 on them and one with numbers 1 to 3 on them. At the start of their turn each team selects a card from each set, one indicating the number of an answer on the category card and one indicating a bonus score of one to three. Should the team give the answer of that number, then they receive the bonus.

12. Four square

Equipment

A squared number-board from 1 to 36, two sets of different coloured squares the same size as the squares on the number-board and a list of general quiz questions.

How to play

Divide into two teams. Decide who goes first. Teams choose a number on the board and a question is asked. If the question is answered correctly then that square is covered over with one of the team's coloured square markers. Each correct answer scores two points and the teams take it in turns to play. The object of the game is to capture four squares in a block and earn a bonus of five points. When all the squares are taken, the score is calculated. Before the game begins the leader may decide that four of the squares will become 'forfeit' squares – these of course will not be known to the children. Should any of these squares be chosen, then the opposing team gain the square and also the play goes to them.

13. Run-around

A quiz run-around can be fun if you have enough space. For example, true or false questions can be asked and areas of the room designated as 'true' and 'false'. Alternatively areas of the room can be numbered, say 1 to 5, and quiz questions may be asked (whose answers are numbers 1 to 5). Children have to run to the correct place; those that go to the wrong place are out.

Scripture verses

Children find it much easier to learn than adults so the more Scripture verses they learn when they are young, the better it is.

GENERAL POINTS

1. Always learn the reference with the verse.

2. Don't learn a verse every week.

3. Make it fun by incorporating it into a game.

4. Put the verse to music.

5. Give children incentives, from time to time, to learn the verse.

6. Put the verse on an activity sheet as a puzzle.

7. Wherever possible use verses which have an application into everyday life. Help the children know how they can use the verses that they learn as a 'sword' to fight against the enemy and as 'food' to feed on.

DISCOVERY GAMES

Learning Scripture verses can be an arduous task, and can become a boring routine for the children. So below are some ways of making the process more fun. Except for the very young, children enjoy an element of competition, so working in teams adds another dimension.

1. Jigsaws

Write out the Scripture verse with the reference on a sheet of card. (This could be in a shape reflective of the verse being used, e.g. a heart, a man, etc.) Cut the card into different shaped pieces (an average of 12 pieces. less for younger children). The aim is to collect all the pieces and to assemble the jigsaw as quickly as possible. The jigsaw could be done on the floor, or on a board which can then be lifted up for ease of visibility.

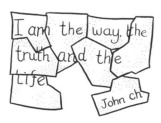

Choose a couple of children to do the jigsaw and others (possibly even the remainder if working with a small group) to collect the pieces and deliver them to those doing the puzzle.

Pieces may be:

a. Hidden under chairs, on leaders, etc.

b. Stuck on the walls around the room.

c. Thrown up in the air (the children scramble for the pieces).

d. Collected by means of a relay. The children line up at one end of the room with a leader who hands them a piece of the jigsaw and they run (hop, skip, bunny jump, walk, crawl, etc.) in turn to deliver them.

e. Collected from a game of 'Pass the Parcel'.

f. Collected by means of a fishing game. Attach paper clips or magnetic tape to the pieces of card and use small magnets to attract the 'fish'.

g. Stuck round a board and the children then take it in turns to fit as many pieces in as possible. Each child is given a set amount of time, e.g. one minute.

2. Wordcards

Write out the Scripture verse and reference on strips of card. Number them. All the above methods can be used to gather the pieces. Then the pieces have to be put in the correct order either on a board, on the floor, or the children holding the pieces have to get themselves in order.

A variation would be to jumble the letters of the words, so that the children have to discover what each word says and then put them in order.

3. Build a wall

Write out the Scripture verse and reference on strips of card. Number them if necessary. Stick each card onto a cardboard box. Discover the verse by building the wall so that the words are in the correct order.

With a small group of children, children's building bricks could be used to build other three dimensional object, e.g. a man, a house.

4. Coded verses

Write out the verse using a code (this is only suitable when the verse is short). The children working on their own, or in small groups, use the code to discover the verse, writing it out as they go.

5. Missing letters

Write out the verse missing out letters, e.g. all the vowels. On small pieces of card write the missing letters. The children have to fill in the gaps. The pieces could be gathered using any of the methods above (see Jigsaws, page 99).

6. Balloon burst

Write the words of the verse on very small pieces of paper and put them into balloons. One at a time, the children try to burst the balloons and collect the words of the verse which will then need to be put in order.

7. Pair 'em up

Write the words of the verse on strips of card which need to be clearly numbered. Write the words again, jumbling the letters. Give these out to the children who have to 'pair 'em up' with the correct words and then discover the verse.

8. Human words

Write the verse on a piece of card or OHP sheet leaving a small number of words out. Divide the children into two teams. One team is given the first word that is missing and have to make the word, 'with their bodies', for the other team to guess. Then change over and continue in the same manner until all the missing words have been discovered. It can be a lot of fun but don't choose too many or words which are too long. A group of children may need an older child or an adult to organise them.

CRAFT ACTIVITIES

1. Illustrated bookmark

2. Memory mobile

Make different shapes with the words of a verse written on them. Construct a mobile using coat hangers, pipe cleaners, etc. Remember, colour will make a lot of difference.

3. Posters/pictures

Younger children enjoy colouring, so use outline letters when preparing these. Older children can design their own posters to illustrate a Scripture verse.

LEARNING METHODS

1. Take it in turns

Get different groups to say the verse, e.g. girls then boys, everyone who has a sister, etc.

2. Stand up/sit down

Divide the children into two groups, e.g. boys and girls. Each group reads alternate words and has to stand up as they read and sit down when they are not. (Alternatives include hand up/hand down, whisper/shout, etc).

3. Rub out a word

Write the verse on a blackboard or whiteboard or alternatively on strips of card which are then stuck onto a board. Either rub out words or remove them as the children become more proficient in saying the verse. (The number that you rub out in one go will depend on the age and ability of the children.) The children should know the verse well by the time that you are left with an empty board.

4. Actions

Put actions to various key words. Say the verse and replace certain words with actions. (Encouraging the children to think about what actions could be used may even increase their understanding of the verse.)

Selecting and appointing children's leaders

Great care needs to be taken when selecting leaders to work with children. Chris and John Leach write in their book, *And For Your Children:*

It so happened in our last church that we had two crises at the same time (that was a good week with only two). The first was that we urgently needed more people to count the collection after services, and the second was that there was no one to look after the babies and toddlers in the creche. The leadership made a policy decision that we could not ask just anyone to count money: they had to be people we knew and trusted, and whose integrity and honesty was beyond question. We would personally approach people whom we had listed as fitting the bill. At the same time we made a general appeal at our Sunday services for anyone who could help with the children to have a word afterwards.

What we had done dawned on us fairly quickly. We had acted as though money was more impor-tant than children. Anyone would do for them, but money had to be handled by the 'right' people lest anything should go wrong.

This situation, typical in so many of our churches, must change. Children need to be treated as VIPs, they deserve the best in spiritual leadership and need to be safeguarded from those who would harm them in any way.

IMPORTANT GUIDELINES

1. A church needs to agree a set policy for the appointment of children's leaders.

   Firstly this will involve a decision on how to discover who might be interested in being involved in the children's work. This could be:

   a. for a church leader or an established chil-dren's worker to make the first contact and approach prospective leaders personally.

   b. for there to be a general appeal given, together with an invitation to meet with those who have responsibility for making appointments.

   c. for a questionnaire to be given to new mem-bers, and also at set intervals to all church members. This would give people the opportunity to evaluate any current ministry/ service in which they are involved within the church, as well as challenging them about possible new areas. This would provide invaluable information when looking for new children's leaders, etc.

   Secondly it is very helpful to go through a set process before *anyone* is allowed to start working with children.

   a. Construct a questionnaire/application form to give to all prospective leaders (see example on page 103).

   b. The Baptist Union suggests a useful five-stage process in their publication *Safe to Grow*. This or something similar could be used.

   Stage One: Treat all would-be workers as job applicants for any position involving contact with children.

   Stage Two: Gain at least one reference from a person who has first-hand knowledge of the volunteer's work with children (or, if they have no previous experience, someone who can at least give a character reference).

   Stage Three: Explore the applicant's experi-ence of working or contact with children in an extended conversation.

   Stage Four: Ask whether the volunteer has any conviction for criminal offences.

   Stage Five: Make appointments conditional on the successful completion of a probationary period.

   (It is also possible to have prospective children's leaders checked by the police, and in this day and age this should be an important con-sideration.)

2. It is helpful to have a document stating the requirements and the responsibilities of chil-dren's leaders. Churches need to decide what they expect from children's leaders and it is helpful for people to carefully consider whether they can meet these requirements before they ever get involved.

3. Give opportunity for people to 'come and see' what happens in a typical children's meeting before they commit themselves to the work.

4. If at all possible avoid parents having to have their own children in their group.

5. Devise an on-going training scheme for those with little or no experience.

   Many people won't get involved in children's work because they feel that they will have to do things for which they don't have the expertise. Experienced leaders need to work alongside newcomers until they have the confidence to operate on their own.

6. Give opportunity for people who may not be able to lead a group but who are happy to be an 'extra pair of hands'.

   Many teenagers fall into this category. While for some this will be a ministry that they want to pursue, others will just see the children's work as an escape route from the adult service. Identify those who are serious about being involved, provide training and give them opportunities to lead parts of the programme as and when appropriate. The aim should be for them to develop to such an extent that they can become fully fledged leaders.

7. Consider drawing up a contract of service for people to sign committing themselves to the work for a set period of time (a minimum time would probably need to be about a year).

   A contract has a number of advantages:

   a. The minds of people who are reluctant to commit themselves to a specific ministry for fear that once they are 'in' there is no way out, are put at rest.

   b. It helps to avoid the problem of people opting out with only a moment's notice.

   c. It helps people to view the job in a serious way.

8. Don't just appoint people out of desperation, the wrong people can be worse than no one at all!

If there are no suitable people or not enough to be children's leaders, then consider not having a separate children's meeting until such time as God provides the right people to do the work.

_____ **CHURCH**

CHILDREN'S WORKERS APPLICATION

Name: _____

Address: _____

_____

_____

_____

Tel no: _____

How long have you been a Christian? _____

Do you believe that the Lord has called you to serve the children in _____ Church? _____

Do you have any experience of working with children? _____

Do you have any experience of working with children in a Christian context? _____

If the answer is yes to the last two questions, please give details. _____

_____

_____

Do you have any particular gifts or talents that you would be prepared to offer to the children's ministry? E.g. artistic, musical, first aid, etc. Please give details. _____

_____

_____

Are you prepared to give priority in your time schedule to any meetings organised by the leadership of the children's ministry? _____

What aspect of the children's ministry do you want to be involved in? (e.g. Sunday groups, midweek clubs, holiday clubs, school assembly team, etc.)
(Insert whatever is appropriate) _____

_____

Are you prepared to work as a member of a team? _____

Is there a particular age group that you would like to work with? _____

Are you prepared to attend recommended training courses? _____

Give the name, address and telephone number of someone who knows you well and would be able to give you a personal reference. What is their relationship to you?

_____

_____

_____

Declaration

You will understand the great responsibility involved in working with children and young people, and the need to ensure their safety.

We therefore ask you to sign the following declaration.

Have you ever been convicted of a criminal offence, or are you at present the subject of criminal charges? (N.B. The disclosure of an offence may not be a bar to your appointment.) YES/NO

If YES, what was the nature of the offence?

_____

_____

_____

_____ Date _____

Signed _____ Date _____

All convictions must be disclosed, as the provision of the Rehabilitation of Offenders Act 1974 does not apply.

Serving not ruling

There is a familiar cry in most church situations – 'we need more leaders, we don't have enough space and where are all the men?' Traditionally children's work tends to be the 'Cinderella' of church life and as a result children's leaders are often regarded as second-rate leaders, seen as child minders rather than having an important spiritual role.

Many people are involved in children's work for all the wrong reasons. These may include the following:

1. There is no one else to do it!

2. Well, it's expected of me; after all, I am a qualified teacher!

3. It's better than having to listen to a boring sermon every week!

4. It's good experience for what God might want me to do in the future.

5. Well, I've always done it!

6. It gives me a great sense of personal satisfaction.

7. I'm too old to be in the Sunday School but not really old enough 'to stay in for the sermon'.

8. I'm not spiritual enough to be involved in any other ministry.

9. I really love children!

QUALIFICATIONS OF CHILDREN'S LEADERS

It is important that leaders:

1. Are called by God.
More often than not God doesn't call the qualified, he qualifies the called. He wants those who will recognise their limitations, maybe even their lack of experience and gifting but who will respond to his call trusting him to provide all that they need (Hebrews 13:21).

2. Share his heart for children.
As Bill Wilson says, 'You can be a teacher for thirty years and have a dozen achievement certificates on your walls, but they are meaningless if you don't have a heart for your class. Do you cry when they cry? Are you touched by their feelings?'

3. Are willing to work not just FOR him but WITH him.
God doesn't just want slaves he wants co-workers. Those who will work under his guidance, co-operating with him, being flexible and doing only those things that they see him doing, just as Jesus did only those things that he saw his Father doing (John 5:19).

4. Put the children's needs before their own.
This involves:

a. Being full of love for the children, even the difficult ones!

b. Identifying with them as fully as possible. Paul said in 1 Corinthians 9:22: 'To the weak I became weak, to win the weak. I have become all things to all men so that by all means I might save some.'

c. Seeing things through the children's eyes. Leaders need to ask God to enable them to see the world through 5-year-old eyes if it is 5-year-olds with whom they are working, and so on.

d. Making every effort to create the right environment so that children feel safe, relaxed and happy.

5. Are 'spiritual', – i.e. their lives are ones of prayer, worship, integrity, etc.
Deuteronomy 4:9 says, 'Only be careful, and watch yourselves closely so that you do not forget the things your eyes have seen . . . Teach them to your children and to their children after them.'

It is vitally important that leaders work out of their relationship with God, that they believe what he says, that they hear him speaking to them, etc. As a result they will have something to share with the children that is 'alive' rather than just a catalogue of facts.

6. Are committed to the church and its vision.
There is a danger that those who are not in total agreement with the vision of the church will try to 'lose' themselves in the children's work where they can work out their own vision. This state of affairs will ultimately have a detrimental effect on the children and will hinder their integration into the body of the church.

Leaders need to be totally committed to the church and be prepared to apply the general vision of the church to the children's work.

7. Are prepared to commit themselves totally to the work.
This involves:

a. The willingness to give time to preparation, to meeting with other leaders and parents, to training as well as to the actual meetings with the children.

b. Perseverance even when the going is tough!

c. Ensuring that they receive spiritual instruction/ teaching at other times if they regularly miss the sermon on a Sunday morning while they are out with the children.

8. Are willing to be accountable.
It is vital that a children's worker is not 'independent' in the work but is prepared to submit their views, ideas, etc., to those who have ultimate responsibility for the work and to be open to correction and discipline.

9. Are willing to learn.
It is important to realise that we never 'make it' as regards the things of God; there are always new things to be learnt. Children's leaders need to be prepared to learn from one another, to learn from the children as well as to take every opportunity to learn from those with greater experience in the work.

10. Are reliable.
We live in a day and age when people are 'in'

and 'out' of things all the time. The children's leader needs to be completely reliable on an on-going basis.

11. Are excellent role models.
Never expect a child to do something which you could not or would not do yourself.

Paul was able to tell the Corinthians to follow his example as he followed the example of Christ. Leaders need to be able to say this to the children that they are working with.

12. Expect great things from God.

RESPONSIBILITIES

Children's leaders have a responsibility to:
1. God.
They need to realise the gravity of their position before God.

Hebrews 13:17 says, 'Obey your leaders and submit to their authority. They keep watch over you as men who will give an account.' Leaders, even those who lead children, will one day have to give an account of what they have done with those for whom they have had responsibility, it's a sobering thought!

Also, in James 3:1 it says, 'Not many of you should presume to be teachers, my brothers, because you know that we who teach will be judged more strictly.'

Children's leaders are teachers of those who are very impressionable, and will be judged accordingly.

2. The children.
God is a God of excellence. When he looked at what he had created at the beginning of time, his assessment of it was that it was very good. Leaders have a responsibility to ensure that his assessment of what they do with the children will be the same.

3. To parents.
The responsibility for both the physical and the spiritual upbringing of children lies in the hands

of the parents. However, the church needs to be a back-up service, working in partnership with parents, sharing expertise and generally supporting them.

N.B. It is important that the role of the parent is never usurped by a children's leader or by the church as a whole.

4. To the church.
Church members need to be helped to see that children are an integral part of the church, that they have great spiritual potential and have a part to play in church life. Often the best people to communicate this are those who are working with the children on a regular basis. This communication may be in a direct way or else through the leadership of the church.

TEAMWORK

All the children's leaders in a church situation need to be working as a team. However, there will probably be a need to divide into 'mini' teams within each department or age group. But whatever the case there are enormous advantages in being part of a team and also pitfalls to be avoided.

Advantages:

1. Mutual support and encouragement.

2. A shared workload.

3. The opportunity to work within one's gifting.

Possible pitfalls:

1. Personal ambition.

2. Competition between members of a team and between different teams.

3. Envy.

4. An independent spirit.

Vital ingredients of good teamwork include:

1. One shared vision, in line with the general vision of the church with the specifics agreed by the church leadership.

2. Good, open and regular communication.

3. Honouring others above yourself, Romans 12:10.

4. One overall leader.

CONCLUSION

In a hundred years' time, it won't matter what my bank balance was, what kind of car I drove or what my clothes were like – but the world may be a better place because I was important in the life of a child (Anon).

Exercise 1

Have you been called by God to work with children? How do you know?

Exercise 2

How is a 5-year-old's world different from yours? (Substitute the age for that of the children with whom you are working.)

ARE 'THEY' BEING SERVED?

Below are some of the main qualifications/qualities of a good children's leader. Assess how you are doing by circling the number that best indicates your experience at this moment in time.

YOU ARE . . .

1. Called by God	0 1 2 3 4 5
2. Sharing his heart for children	0 1 2 3 4 5
3. Willing to work not just FOR him but WITH him	0 1 2 3 4 5
4. Putting the children's needs before your own	0 1 2 3 4 5
5. 'Spiritual', i.e. your life is one of prayer, worship, integrity, etc.	0 1 2 3 4 5
6. Committed to the church and its vision	0 1 2 3 4 5
7. Prepared to commit yourself totally to the work	0 1 2 3 4 5
8. Willing to be accountable	0 1 2 3 4 5
9. Willing to learn	0 1 2 3 4 5
10. Reliable	0 1 2 3 4 5
11. An excellent role model	0 1 2 3 4 5
12. Expecting great things from God	0 1 2 3 4 5

The above is an exercise that probably needs to be repeated at regular intervals since circumstances change all the time.

Those areas for which you get a low score obviously need some attention. This may involve some practical things being done and some concentrated prayer.

EVALUATION SHEET FOR CHILDREN'S LEADERS

Assess how much time you spend doing the following:

1 = not much time at all 5 = quite a bit of time

PASTORAL CARE

Praying with individuals within your group	1	2	3	4	5
Visiting them in their homes	1	2	3	4	5
Finding out what things they like to do	1	2	3	4	5
Listening to their news	1	2	3	4	5
Advising them over difficult situations	1	2	3	4	5
Remembering what they told you the previous week	1	2	3	4	5
Remembering about their families and birthdays	1	2	3	4	5
Asking God what he wants for a particular child	1	2	3	4	5
Noticing if they seem worried or upset	1	2	3	4	5
Noticing if they are missing	1	2	3	4	5

TEACHING THEM ABOUT

Who God is (What he is like)	1	2	3	4	5
What God can do	1	2	3	4	5
How much God loves them	1	2	3	4	5
How God wants to use them	1	2	3	4	5
Enemy attacks and how to deal with them	1	2	3	4	5
The importance of prayer	1	2	3	4	5
The importance of knowing God's word	1	2	3	4	5
Sin and repentance	1	2	3	4	5
How to live to please God	1	2	3	4	5
Relationships with one another	1	2	3	4	5
Being a part of the church	1	2	3	4	5
Who the Holy Spirit is	1	2	3	4	5
Spiritual gifts	1	2	3	4	5

EVANGELISM

Training the children to share their faith	1	2	3	4	5
Encouraging children to bring friends	1	2	3	4	5
Praying for children who are not Christians	1	2	3	4	5
Taking an interest in schools' work	1	2	3	4	5
Inviting neighbours' children to meetings	1	2	3	4	5
Arranging social events suitable for guests	1	2	3	4	5
Organising an outreach activity	1	2	3	4	5

SOCIAL INTERACTION

Sharing news together	1	2	3	4	5
Spending leisure time together	1	2	3	4	5
Making sure no one is left out	1	2	3	4	5
Sharing meals together	1	2	3	4	5
Working on a project together	1	2	3	4	5
Inviting older members of the church to 'share'	1	2	3	4	5
Encouraging older children to talk to younger ones	1	2	3	4	5

TEAM WORK QUESTIONNAIRE

So when each separate part works as it should, the whole body grows and builds itself up through love. (Ephesians 4:16)

God is committed to people working together to accomplish all that they can for him. He wants his people to be in a place where they can work out of their strengths/gifts/abilities rather than being forced, as often happens in children's ministry, to do everything whether they have the necessary gifts/abilities or not. He knows how important it is for us to succeed and the best place to do this is to be functioning in a team, doing those things that we have the learned skills or gifts to do. This is the ideal.

Unfortunately, however, the world in which we live is far from ideal, particularly, it seems, when we start considering children's ministry! There are times when we are all called upon to be a 'jack of all trades' but there is a need to work in a team context whenever possible. In most situations the best way of viewing those involved in the children's ministry in a particular church is as one team, divided down into mini-teams catering for the various groups into which children may be divided. Teams can vary in size right down to two people. However big or small the team, it is important to discover what roles are being fulfilled in the team and which are not. This means that if there are gaps that can be identified, then the kind of people that are needed will be obvious – recruitment and specific prayer will be easier.

Below are the main roles necessary in a good, balanced team. For each of the roles, circle the number on the 0 to 5 scale which best describes your level of strength/gifting. Each member of the team needs to do this exercise and then there needs to be a sharing of the results.

1. Leader/Co-ordinator	0 1 2 3 4 5
2. Teacher	0 1 2 3 4 5
3. Intercessor	0 1 2 3 4 5
4. Evangelist	0 1 2 3 4 5
5. Encourager	0 1 2 3 4 5
6. Prophet (Visionary)	0 1 2 3 4 5
7. Administrator/Strategist	0 1 2 3 4 5
8. Pastor/Counsellor	0 1 2 3 4 5
9. Creative	
a. arts (music, drama, art)	0 1 2 3 4 5
b. thinker (ideas)	0 1 2 3 4 5
10. Worship leader	0 1 2 3 4 5
11. 'Dogsbody'!	0 1 2 3 4 5
12. 'Handy man/woman'!	0 1 2 3 4 5

Visual aids

A visual aid is anything visual that will aid communication. It will never turn a useless communicator into a brilliant one overnight but used in the right way by the right person it can greatly improve the quality of communication.

WHY USE VISUAL AIDS?

1. We remember far more of what we see than what we hear. After fifteen months a person will remember 28 per cent of facts which are taught verbally, but up to 78 per cent of what he is taught verbally when accompanied by visual aids.

2. They aid concentration. They provide a focus for listeners.

3. They have enormous attention-gaining potential.

4. God used them, e.g. a rainbow (Genesis 9:1ff), bread and wine (John 13), a child (Matthew 18:2).

Some of the methods of teaching (see section on Creative Teaching, page 45) are in themselves a visual stimulus.

However, below are some types of pre-prepared visual aids to accompany 'straight' storytelling or teaching.

PICTURES

(This is the most obvious form of visual aid.)

Overhead projector pictures

Advantages
- Easy to store.
- Can be used with both large and small groups (depending on the screen size).
- Can be traced, photocopied or printed from clipart or scanned pictures on a computer (There are a number of books produced from which you can do this. See the Resources section on page 117.)
- Easy to see.

Disadvantages
- Limited range of colours.
- Screen is in a different place to the storyteller, therefore there is limited eye contact.

(Practical tips: When drawing pictures on OHP acetate sheets draw on the front and colour on the back. This will avoid black outlines smudging into other colours. Store pictures with paper between them to avoid them sticking together, particularly if left in a hot place.)

Pictures drawn on single sheets of card or paper or on a roll of paper

Advantages
- If brightly coloured they can be more visually appealing than OHP pictures.
- The storyteller can hold them, so maintaining eye contact with the listeners.
- They can be used in any situation, without the need for additional equipment.

Disadvantages
- Very time consuming to prepare.
- Difficult to store.
- They can only be used with relatively small groups.

BIBLE STORY BOOKS

These are readily available but are, of course, only suitable for very small groups.

FLANNELGRAPHS

These were very popular in the past and still have some novelty value today. They are expensive to buy, however, and can only be used with small groups. A similar alternative would be to use a metal board and attach the pictures with the use of magnetic tape.

OBJECTS

These are freely available but have limited use with large groups.

VIDEOS

More and more good children's Bible-based videos are being produced, but because children have become used to watching videos as an everyday activity, they don't seem to have the same impact (particularly with older children) as they once did.

(Practical Tips: Ensure that your equipment is working well, that the video is at the right starting point and that you have watched it beforehand to check its suitability.)

COMPUTER-GENERATED PRESENTATIONS

Using software programmes such as PowerPoint and clipart/video images, etc., it is possible to produce some excellent visual aids. However, to do this does involve not only a fair degree of computer competence but also some expensive equipment. This will no doubt become more and more popular as time goes on.

RESOURCE COLLECTIONS

The preparation of some visual aids can be very time consuming and it is important therefore that they are stored carefully for future use. A church resource collection that is well catalogued and available for those involved in the children's ministry to use can be a huge asset, saving both time and money.

It is also useful to find out if there are people in the church who have artistic or computer skills who would be prepared to produce visual aids for use in the children's ministry. This can be a good way of involving people who would otherwise never have anything to do with the children. In addition you could end up with a great resources collection!

Exercise 1

Do some research to discover what books are available which might be helpful in the production of visual aids. Try and discover if there are church members who would be prepared to do illustrations, etc.

Exercise 2

Decide where the church's resources collection could be kept and catalogued. What resources would you want in your collection?

Watch your language!

Words are the basis of communication and as Christians we have a very definite Christian vocabulary. Church generally is very 'word' orientated and this can cause problems for those who have limited reading ability, but for children and new Christians even the vocabulary can be difficult, if not impossible, to understand. Apart from this affecting teaching sessions, etc., it can also make worship difficult. If songs are full of words that those singing cannot understand, then only limited worship is possible.

There are a number of mistakes that it is easy to make in children's work and the choice of words and tone of voice can 'make or break' a session:

1. 'Speaking down' to children with a patronising tone of voice.

2. Using language that is not age appropriate to the children.

3. Using Christian 'jargon' and/or biblical words that the children don't understand. It is obviously very important that children do become familiar with words that are used primarily in a Christian context but it is vital that adequate explanation is given as and when these words are used. For instance, once when I was teaching about the Holy Spirit one child interrupted and said that her dad drunk 'spirits' at the pub, was that the same?

Exercise 1

The following are words which are frequently used and which children need to understand. Take each word in turn and think about how you would explain it to the children with whom you work.

1. ANOINTED
2. EXALT
3. HOLY
4. SIN
5. MERCY
6. GRACE
7. SAVED
8. SOUL
9. WORSHIP
10. GLORY
11. SACRIFICE
12. FORGIVEN
13. HEART
14. SALVATION

Exercise 2

Make a list of 10 words that describe God. Ask the children in your group to do the same. Notice the differences between the two lists.

Leader's list	Children's list
1. _____	1. _____
2. _____	2. _____
3. _____	3. _____
4. _____	4. _____
5. _____	5. _____
6. _____	6. _____
7. _____	7. _____
8. _____	8. _____
9. _____	9. _____
10. _____	10. _____

Worksheets

In these days of photocopies and computers, worksheets, or activity/puzzle sheets as they are sometimes called, can be easily produced and are an extremely valuable resource in children's ministry.

USES

Worksheets can be used in a number of different ways:

1. As a reinforcer of a particular teaching point or story.

2. As a discussion starter, therefore as something to initiate teaching.

3. As an activity which is hopefully both fun and enjoyable.

4. As a Bible reading aid.

As with everything, children will quickly get bored if they are presented with a worksheet every time that they meet together. Use them sparingly to gain the greatest effect. Also, don't just use them to keep children occupied at times when you have completed the main programme, e.g. when waiting for parents to collect their children, this has the effect of devaluing them.

WHAT KIND OF WORKSHEET?

It is really important to have a clear idea of the purpose of any sheet that is given to children. Obviously if you construct your own it is easier to gear it specifically to your group and what you want to achieve. However, there are many excellent books available containing sheets which can be just as useful (see the Resources section on page 117).

Worksheets produced on a computer using desktop publishing, a wordsearch/crossword construction programme and possibly some of the enormous amount of clipart that is now available can give a professional look but can also appear 'sterile' and like something that a child might be given in school. Alternatively a 'hand' produced sheet can appear much more inviting but, if not done well, can look 'scruffy' and not worth bothering about.

TIPS FOR CONSTRUCTING A WORKSHEET

1. Decide on the purpose of the worksheet: what do you want it to achieve? How will it be used, e.g. as part of a session or as a take home sheet?

2. Take into consideration the ages and abilities of the children. The ability levels of any group will probably cover a wide range, making it important to include simpler things and also something which will 'stretch' the more able children.

3. Don't put too much on a page otherwise it will look cluttered and may give the children a sense of not quite knowing where to start.

4. Ensure that any handwriting is readable. It doesn't necessarily have to be big but it does have to be clear!

5. Don't write entirely in capital letters, they are much more difficult for children to read.

6. Use a ruler to draw lines unless they are meant to be 'artistic' looking.

7. If constructing puzzles by hand, use squared paper for grids.

8. Use black ink – it gives the best quality when photocopied.

9. Ensure that spaces left for children to fill in are large enough, bearing in mind that children's writing tends to be quite a lot bigger than adults.

10. Use a variety of different activities.

    These could include wordsearches, crosswords, mazes, code-breakers, spot the difference, join the dots, true or false questions, pictures to colour, verses to look up in the Bible, questions (both factual and 'how does this apply to your life' types), space for personal testimony/prayer requests, etc.

11. Check the finished sheet well so as to avoid unnecessary mistakes. It is easy to miss mistakes when you have been working on something because you tend to see what you think it should be, so it can be useful to find someone who will 'proof read'/check sheets for you.

12. Ensure that there is a good balance between 'words' and pictures.

13. Ensure that the copy quality is good.

14. Involve others, who have the necessary skills and time, in the production of sheets. There may be people who would never get involved with a children's group but who, in consultation with the leader, would be more than happy to produce an occasional worksheet.

Exercise 1

Buy a couple of children's puzzle books and make a list of all the different kinds of puzzles that are contained in them.

Exercise 2

Prepare a worksheet, for the age group with which you work, on the subject of prayer. Discuss the good and bad points of your finished result with other children's leaders. How could it have been improved?

Reference books

CASTLEMAN, Robbie. *Parenting in the Pew*, IVP, 1993.

CLUTTERHAM, Terry. *The Adventure Begins*, SU/CPAS, 1996

CRAY, Jackie. *Seen and Heard*, Monarch

LANE, Vann. *Children of Revival*, Destiny Image, 1998

LAYTON, Dian. *Soldiers with Little Feet*, Destiny Image (Revival Press), 1989

LEACH, Chris and John. *And for Your Children*, Monarch, 1994

LEFEVER, M. *Learning Styles*, Kingsway, 1998

PORTER, David. *Children at Play*, Kingsway, 1989

PORTER, David. *Children at Risk*, Kingsway, 1998

POWERPACK. *Training Up Children of the Word*, Powerpack Trust, 21A Mountside, Guildford, Surrey GU2 5JD, 2000

PRICE, Alan. *Children in Renewal*, Kevin Mayhew, 2000

RAYMOND, Gillian. *Dear God, Can You Wink?* SU, 1995

VAN NESS, Patricia. *Transforming Bible Study with Children*, Abingdon Press, 1991

WALTERS, David. *Kids in Combat*, Good News Fellowship Ministries, 1989

WILSON, Bill. *Whose Child is it Anyway?* (Originally published by Word Books in 1992 under the title *Streets of Pain*.)

Resource books

ACTIVITY/PUZZLE SHEETS

Instant Art for Bible Worksheets, Books 3, 4 and 5, Kevin Mayhew

Instant Art for Bible Themes Worksheets, Books 2 and 3, Kevin Mayhew

Instant Art for Bible Fun, Book 2, Kevin Mayhew

Instant Art for Bible People and Scenes, Kevin Mayhew

Instant Art for Bible Puzzles, Book 2, Kevin Mayhew

Instant Art for Bible Colouring, Kevin Mayhew

Instant Art for Pre-school Bible Activity Sheets, Books 1 and 2, Kevin Mayhew

DE VRIES, B. *101 Bible Activity Sheets*, Baker Book House
(ISBN:0-8010-2931-7), 1993

The Beginner's Bible Amazing Stories Maze Book (ISBN 0-679-87528-X), 1995

Following a Star (A Palm Tree Puzzle Book), Kevin Mayhew

The Welcoming Party (A Palm Tree Puzzle Book), Kevin Mayhew

ART AND CRAFT

COPSEY, K. *Here's One I Made Earlier*, Scripture Union

PRICE, S. *100 Craft Ideas for Children*, Kingsway

Instant Art for Bible Action Models, Kevin Mayhew

The Bumper Book of Instant Art for Bible Cut-outs, Kevin Mayhew

Instant Art for Pre-School Colouring, Books 1, 2 and 3, Kevin Mayhew

DRAMA

Play on Words, Kevin Mayhew, 2000

HOPWOOD, D. *Telling Tales*, CPAS, 1997

SCHER, A. & VERALL, C. *100+ Ideas for Drama*, Heinemann

GAMES

GOODLAND, P. *Over 300 Games for All Occasions*, Scripture Union, 1985

PHILLIPS, B. *The World's Best Collection of Great Games*,
  Harvest House Publishers, 1998

PINCHBECK, L. *Theme Games*, Scripture Union, 1993

HOLIDAY CLUB MATERIAL

CARTER, A. & HARDWICK, J. *The Ultimate Holiday Club Guide*,
  Bible Reading Fellowship, 1995

Megaquest, Scripture Union

Storykeepers, Scripture Union

Going Bananas!, Scripture Union

Chatterbox, Scripture Union

MAGIC

Books and tricks available from Tricks for Truth, 91 Green Street, Middleton, Manchester M24 2TB

MEMORY VERSES

52 Ways to Teach Memory Verses, Rainbow Books

CURRIER, M. *Bible Memory Activity Book*, Baker Book House, 1994

MISSION

Children Just Like Me, Dorling Kindersley.

LEONARD, C. *Children on the Edge*, Tear Fund and Scripture Union, 1995 (Stories of children from around the world)

The Great Kidmission, Gospel Light (ISBN 0-8307-1761-1), 1996

People Who Changed the World (A series of books, each featuring a famous missionary), OM Publishing

You Can Change the World, OM Publishing

You Too Can Change the World, OM Publishing

52 Ways to Teach Missions, Rainbow Books, 1996

The Mission Zone, OMF/Christian Focus, 1999

MOVEMENT AND DANCE

Books of choreographed dances available from Marie Bensley, Sunset Gate, St. Audries, Taunton, Somerset TA4 4EA

PRAISE AND WORSHIP

Powerpack Praise (Music Book available from the Powerpack Trust)

Mighty Warrior (Praise and worship cassette and music book) ICC 25120

Worship the King (Praise and worship cassette and music book) ICC 16420

Kidsource, Kevin Mayhew

PRAYER

52 Ways to Teach Children to Pray, Rainbow Books, 1991

PRAYER TOOLS: Esther Network International 854, Conniston Rd., West Palm Beach, Florida 33405-2131, USA

DYER, J. *100 Creative Prayer Ideas*, Kingsway, 1999

FULLER, Cheri. *When Children Pray*, Multnomah Publishers

MERRELL, J. *One Hundred and One Ideas for Creative Prayer*, Scripture Union, 1995

OSBORNE, Rick. *Teaching Your Child How to Pray*, Moody Press, 1997

POWERPACK. Training Up Prayer Warriors, Powerpack Trust, 21A Mountside, Guildford, Surrey GU2 5JD

PUPPETS

Puppet Power, Kevin Mayhew, 2000

QUIZZES

GREEN, R. *Over 120 Quizzes For All Occasions*, Scripture Union, 1987

CHEWTER, R. & M. *Quiz Resource Book*, Scripture Union, 1996

Instant Art for Bible Quizzes, Kevin Mayhew

TEACHING IDEAS

NEILANDS, L. *50 Five-minute Stories*, Kingsway, 1996

NEILANDS, L. *50 Stories for Special Occasions Throughout the Year*, Kingsway

RELF, S. *100 Instant Children's Talks*, Kingsway

VISUAL AIDS

Acetate Masters for Palm Tree Bible Stories, Books 1 and 2, Kevin Mayhew

How to Cheat at Visual Aids (Old Testament), Scripture Union, 1997

How to Cheat at Visual Aids (New Testament), Scripture Union, 1996

Acetate Masters (individual stories), The Powerpack Trust